A MEDICAL SCIENTIST
EXAMINES THE
LIFE OF JESUS

A MEDICAL SCIENTIST EXAMINES THE
LIFE OF JESUS

A Series of Studies by
Peter Elwood

PETER ELWOOD

Library of Congress Control Number:		2019903224
ISBN:	Hardcover	978-1-5434-9483-9
	Softcover	978-1-5434-9482-2
	eBook	978-1-5434-9481-5

Print information available on the last page.

Rev. date: 03/21/2019

To order additional copies of this book, contact:
Xlibris
800-056-3182
www.Xlibrispublishing.co.uk
Orders@Xlibrispublishing.co.uk
792869

I have loved to hear my Lord spoken of, and wherever I have seen the print of His shoe in the earth, there I have coveted to set my foot too.

—Mr Stand-Fast, *Pilgrim's Progress*

CONTENTS

THE VIRGIN BIRTH OF JESUS

This aspect of Jesus has been more sharply attacked recently than perhaps any other. For most Christians, it is accepted as 'a matter of faith'—after all, how could there be any evidence of a matter so private as conception and parentage? Close reading of the text, however, will indicate that Mary's story is totally credible; and any other explanation is unacceptable.

The uniqueness of Jesus Christ: The virgin birth is just one of many aspects of the uniqueness of Jesus. Everything about Jesus gives evidence that he was utterly different to every other man who has ever lived. Conception without a human father is consistent with his deity, but birth by a virgin is only one of the many aspects of his uniqueness. It is, however, an essential aspect of his person because in no other way could God and man be united equally in a single being.

The Word became flesh: The name for Jesus used by John in his gospel record is of interest. At one level, it can imply that the 'communication' from God became a man or the 'message' from God became a human being. Look at it this way: I am what I am and you are who you are because of our genes. Coded into the genes within every cell in my body is an incredible amount of information, estimated by some as equivalent to several complete series of *Encyclopaedia Britannica* or about 12 feet of library shelf. Did the second person of the Godhead, the Word, code Himself into Mary's genetic structure, giving information that led to the God-man, Jesus Christ?

The conception of Mary: Luke wrote the third gospel in our New Testament, and he claims (Luke 1: 1) to have investigated everything to do with Jesus very carefully. Because Luke was a doctor, Mary would have found it acceptable to be questioned by him about her conception and her pregnancy. Luke also remarks that Mary's memory was good and she had thought much about all these events 'and had kept them in her heart' (19 and 51).

Luke commences his account of Mary's pregnancy by introducing the reader to an elderly, childless, and religious couple, Elizabeth and Zecharias. He also tells us that this was a very special time for Zecharias. He was a priest and had been selected to perform some very special tasks in the Temple in Jerusalem, a privilege that came to a man only once. In fact, these two people, Zecharias and Elizabeth, come over in Luke's narrative as austere and rather unapproachable— the very last couple to whom a young girl would go if she were in any kind of trouble.

Luke records that Elizabeth, Zechariah's wife, had become pregnant. Perhaps this was somewhat embarrassing for her. After all, she was elderly. Also, her husband's special religious duties in Jerusalem should perhaps have been occupying his full attention! Her pregnancy was certainly no matter for gossip, and Luke remarks that Elizabeth hid herself and remained in seclusion (24). The relatives in distant Nazareth were unlikely to have known anything about all this.

Luke now turns to Mary, a cousin of Elizabeth, and records her story. She claimed that an angel had told her that she would become pregnant by a divine agency. Mary's response to the angel had been very natural: 'Nonsense! How could this be—I have not known a man?' (34). Mary then went on to tell Luke that the angel had then told her that Elizabeth was six months pregnant (36).

Put yourself in Mary's shoes. How would you have responded? The text states that Mary was troubled by what the angel was saying. I guess that Mary's concern increased sharply as the angel went on. *What does this mean that no man will be involved, and what about the neighbours? What will they think? And Joseph? When he finds that I am pregnant, will he believe me?*

And then the angel slipped in a remark about cousin Elizabeth being pregnant (36). What on earth had a pregnancy by another woman to do with what was to the angel was saying would happen to her? Mary's distress was probably increasing throughout the angel's message.

And yet, there is an element of calmness in the final remark by Mary: 'I am the Lord's servant, be it onto me as you have said' (.38). Behind her distress, had it suddenly occurred to Mary that the angel had given her one fact that could be checked? See Elizabeth and resolve the doubt: angelic vision or bad dream?

Mary's journey: Luke then records that Mary went immediately to see Elizabeth (39). That was quite a remarkable thing for her to do. Nazareth was about 100 miles from Jerusalem—a strange journey for a girl to make and apparently alone, all to meet an elderly, childless, and very religious woman, married to a priest on active duty at the Temple in Jerusalem? Remarkable—even bizarre!

Surely, this is just about the very last thing that a young girl would have done had she behaved improperly and feared she might be pregnant. Surely, she would have waited for a month, or several months, until she was certain as to whether or not she was indeed pregnant.

On the other hand, if Mary's story is true, if she had indeed been told that she would bear a child by divine intervention, then she would be most likely to go to Elizabeth to check the likely truth of the message of the angel. After all, the information about Elizabeth's pregnancy was the one single fact given to her that could be checked. That journey to Jerusalem was therefore either a foolish and pointless action a most natural response possible in the circumstances.

Mary told Luke that her visit to Elizabeth had lasted three months and
that she then returned home to Nazareth (56). No doubt she remained
with Elizabeth until there were definite signs of pregnancy, perhaps
'quickening' at about twelve weeks (56). She then knew that she would
have to face the gossip and the snide remarks from neighbours back
home in Nazareth. And what about her fiancé? Would he ever believe
her story?

Nothing is said about those three months. And why three months?
One reason may be that the poor girl needed counselling. These two
were godly women, and counselling by the older woman must have
been an immense help to Mary in strengthening her resolve and giving
her courage to return home to face the neighbours and her fiancé.

In addition, although at one level Mary will by now have believed the
message from the angel, doubts may well have lingered. And so she
waited for one month, then a second, and a third, by which time there
may also have been quickening. Then, her resolve strengthened, she
left for home.

An important time mark: Luke records that after Mary had left,
Elizabeth gave birth to a son (57). Pregnancy then, as now, lasted nine
months; and this period of time is totally accounted for by the six
months at the time of the annunciation by the angel to Mary (36) plus
the three months of Mary's stay with Elizabeth.

The Significance of the Time Marks Given in Luke's Account

You shall become pregnant[1] . . . Elizabeth is <u>six months</u> pregnant[2]'

6 + 3 = 9 Months

Mary went immediately to Elizabeth[3] . . . Mary stayed <u>three months</u>[4]

after Mary had left Elizabeth was delivered[5]

1) Luke 1: 31; 2) Luke 1: 36; 3) Luke 1:
39; 4) Luke 1: 56; 5) Luke 1: 57

This means that the full nine months of Elizabeth's pregnancy is accounted for. Mary's claim that she had left Nazareth immediately after the angel had spoken to her is validated, and she therefore had not waited for any signs of pregnancy to appear.

Again, if Mary's story had not been true, if it had been a mere cover-up for some affair, surely, she would have waited for some signs of pregnancy. After all, in the nature of things, there is always a fair chance that an affair will not lead to a pregnancy.

Yet the story gives no opportunity for delay. And to repeat an earlier point, the old and childless Elizabeth was the very last kind of person Mary would have gone to for help had she been in trouble.

On the other hand, if her story was true, then Elizabeth was the *only* person Mary would have wanted to see so that she could check the one testable fact in the message of the angel.

Just picture Mary on that journey, driven by distress, 100 miles of unknown territory, some of it hostile! Picture her having to ask directions repeatedly and find lodging along the way. And then picture her on arrival with Elizabeth: 'Thrilled to see you, and marvellous about your pregnancy . . . and just imagine, I'm going to have a baby too!'

No way! Mary will have had no such reaction. Rather, she will probably have been overcome with dread at seeing Elizabeth. 'So it is true after all. How can I face it, the neighbours, and Joseph?'

Joseph: We have to turn to Matthew to get the story from Joseph's point of view. Matthew had been a tax inspector, and he knew the wiles and deceits of men. Yet he states that Joseph was a 'just' man (Matt. 1: 19).

Of course, Joseph didn't believe Mary's story about an angel. Women just don't get pregnant that way! And so it took a visit from an angel to convince him.

But notice how Matthew records this: Joseph was considering divorce on the grounds of Mary's unfaithfulness (19, 20). He was a kindly man and intended to do this privately to cause Mary as little distress as possible, but immediately the thought entered his mind, an angel appeared.

It is as if the Holy Spirit would not allow any distrust within the holy family. So as soon as Joseph had a dishonourable thought about Mary, the angel intervened and cried, 'Stop!'

One, however, might question why a second angelic visitation was necessary. Surely, it would have been far more reasonable, and more economical, for God to have sent one angel to see them both together. This would have avoided Joseph's misunderstanding and the upset this must have caused both him and Mary.

Indeed, had Joseph been in on it all from the start (or before it all started!), he would undoubtedly have stuck by Mary and he could have been an enormous support to her. All no doubt true, but consider what the neighbours would have thought! 'Some story those two have concocted! What a crude attempt at a cover-up for their misbehaviour!'

Conclusion: The central truth of Christianity is the deity of Jesus. His origin by virgin birth is totally in keeping with his being God and man united in one person. Indeed, virgin conception is the only way that a union between God and man could be achieved without compromising the integrity of either. His virgin birth is also consistent with all the other pieces of evidence of His deity.

However, an acceptance of the virgin birth of Jesus is not a blind leap in the dark. There is evidence in the written records; and while other explanations for Mary's pregnancy have been suggested, none of these have any ring of truth. Most imply that Mary was a liar. One hesitates to even write down these alternative explanations.

Furthermore, Luke 1: 35 links the involvement of the Holy Spirit within Mary with the deity of her child: 'Because of this He will be called the Son of God'. To reject the virgin conception would thus seem to be a rejection of the deity of Jesus Christ.

So Why the Virgin Birth?

1. The Christian message is all about a relationship between God and men, and the gospel starts with the union of God and man in Jesus Christ. The Christian message has been summed up as the descent of God to enable the ascent of man.
2. The Christian gospel is all about 'mediation' between a holy God and sinful men. Job cried out in his agony: 'Oh that there were someone who could put a hand upon us both and bring us together' (Job 9: 33). This is exactly what Jesus Christ can do, being fully God and fully man.
3. God is infinitely pure and holy, and the Bible says that God cannot so much as look upon sin. Man is sinful he can neither lift himself up to God nor cleanse himself and stand before a pure God. The Christian message is that God has come down to man; and in the God-man Jesus, we can be lifted up to God. Our sins can be forgiven; and we can be covered by the purity, the righteousness, of Jesus Christ.

> *Jesus, Thy blood and righteousness, My beauty are, my glorious dress: 'Midst flaming worlds, in these arrayed, With joy shall I lift up my head.* (von Zinzendorf, 1739)

4. A key element in salvation is redemption, a concept that is taken from the slave market. If a person had lost his freedom or his inheritance, this could be bought back. But only a blood relative could redeem, and our old word *kinsman* is in Hebrew 'one who can redeem'. To be our Redeemer, Jesus had first to become our kinsman.
5. The Christian has a High Priest who knows and understands, not just because as God, He is all-knowing but also because He was here. He learned through the things He suffered (Heb. 5: 8), and so He fitted Himself to be merciful and understanding, able to show compassion on the weak and needy (Heb. 5: 1–6).

6. Jesus himself warned that he would conduct the final judgement of men; and when referring to judgement, He referred to Himself as 'the Son of Man' (John 5: 27, NIV). That is, by being man, by living on this earth and by facing all the temptations and difficulties we face, Jesus prepared himself to be our judge. Because he is God, he has the right to judge; and because he is man, he is fitted to judge. There will be no fooling him in that day and no saying that he does not understand! He knows and understands—he was here!

HIS EARLY LIFE

Very little is said about the early life of Jesus. A very few incidents and the general comment that 'He grew in wisdom and in favour with God and man' (Luke 2: 40,52, NIV). Clearly the gospels are a record of the Saviour of the world and not a biography of Jesus of Nazareth.

After childbirth, a Jewish mother went through three ceremonies.

Circumcision: The covenant and indicated subjection to the law. Jesus had come to fulfil the law; and so it was fully appropriate that he, who had given the law to man, was circumcised by the hand of a man.

Redemption: The Jewish ceremony that most closely corresponds to our service of 'thanksgiving' for a child was the ancient ceremony of 'redemption'. This will have taken place during the same visit to the temple as Mary's purification. In the ceremony, the mother will have solemnly handed her infant to one of the priests; and the priest, after a prayer of thanksgiving, will have handed the child back to the mother. This all symbolised two facts: first, that children are a gift, on loan from God; and secondly, the ceremony will have carried the warning that the parents will one day have to give account of their parenting to God. All this was especially meaningful in the case of Jesus, the saviour of men—God's gift to men, but a gift for which we will have to give account one day.

Purification: The third ceremony on that visit by Mary to the temple was her 'purification' (echoed in the Anglican ceremony of 'churching' women after childbirth). The woman offered a lamb 'for her cleansing' (Lev. 12); but if she were poor, two turtledoves would suffice. Is it not incredible that Mary, having carried 'the Holy One of God', went through this (Luke 2: 24); and is it not most poignant that having carried the One through whom all things were made, she made the offering for the poor?

Of course, it had to be so. At one level, Mary knew who her child was, yet her relationship with Him could not be normal and uninhibited had she fully appreciated who He was. And everything later shows that their relationship was loving and caring—the very best a human relationship could be. And it was so with the disciples and with the common people. He had to learn through experience (Heb. 5: 8); and had folk fully realised who He is, they would have been paralysed, and normal relationships would have been impossible! The writer to the Hebrews gives a marvellous light on this when he states, 'His flesh was a veil'. On the one hand, his flesh was a protection for men so that they could touch and handle him and even, on one occasion, strike him. His flesh shielded men from the full glory of God (see Col. 2: 9, NIV).

The home in Nazareth: And eventually the child will have returned to the family home in Nazareth, and there he increased in wisdom and stature and in favour with God and man (Luke 2: 52). The Jews taught that there are eight stages of development from infancy to maturity; and they taught that in each stage, there are clear duties and responsibilities both for parents and for children. How different this was to the casual, indulgent attitude that is the usual today? The emphasis then was on responsibilities while the emphasis today is on 'rights'.

A Jewish home was, and still is, marked by many things but chiefly by the fact that the word of God was, and still is, central. The Jewish Rabbi Lord Jacobowitz was asked how the Jews had remained a separate nation, despite being scattered and persecuted repeatedly beyond any other nation. It is because the word of God is central in every Jewish home, he replied. Their commentators spoke of the scriptures as 'life moulding'. And so, in the home of every Jewish child, there would have been a tremendous emphasis on the word of God, with

- morning and evening prayers;
- grace before and after meals;
- special meals, especially the Sabbath meal;
- the mezuzah on the doorposts, containing a passage of scripture and touched by everyone who went in or out; and
- holy days, which we have downgraded to holidays!

And so a Jewish child will have grown up in an atmosphere of love and value—a gift, on loan from God, with the parents responsible to God for their treatment and for their instruction of the child and the child accountable for his/her behaviour and all the time, regular exposure, and instruction in the word of God.

The mother had responsibility for the very early teaching of the child. But once the child could read, the father took on the responsibility of teaching scripture. A tremendous emphasis was put on memory training, and long passages of scripture were memorised. Every child was given a 'birthday verse', containing the letters of his/her name; and from earliest days, this verse was memorised.

At 5–6 years, the child went to school in the synagogue. One of the early writers states that the aim in school was 'children are to be kept from all contact with vice, they are to be trained in gentleness and in truthfulness, and there is to be an avoidance of all that might lead to indelicate thoughts'. Quaint? And likely to be unacceptable today! Yet how about putting that as a notice above our TV sets and enforcing it with our children?

The study of the scriptures in the synagogue with children will have commenced in the book of Leviticus. Imagine! Few of us could preach from Leviticus apart at most from two or three chapters! But isn't it intensely moving to think of the child Jesus learning

- about the sacrifices, which He would fulfil in His own body;
- about the festivals that would be fulfilled in His own work; and
- about the prophecies that spoke of Him and His work?

And so, the child grew in wisdom and stature and in favour with God and man, and the divine record sums up the early life of Jesus by stating this twice and adding the grace of God was upon Him.

The visit to the temple: At the age of 13, a bar mitzvah was held, and a Jewish boy became 'a child of the covenant'. From then on, he was able to play a full part in Jewish ceremonies. And so, at about this age, Jesus was taken up to the Temple in Jerusalem. He will have journeyed with the crowds; and as they approached Jerusalem, they will have chanted some of the psalms together—the so-called songs of ascent. In front of them the city, with the temple mound and crowning it all, the magnificent gleaming white marble building, the temple.

How thrilling this must have been for any lad. I will never forget my first visit to Jerusalem. It was early morning; and as I walked through the Damascus gate into the Old City, I was overcome with emotion as I thought of how I was walking where He had once walked.

But what did they talk about? Of course, it is conjecture; but I wonder, did Mary tell the lad Jesus all about his previous visit to the temple? He had been only 8 days old, and she had presented him to the priest and had received Him back, a sacred trust from God. And did she tell him of Simeon and his talk of a sword that would pierce her heart? And had she then gone back in time and told the young Jesus of the angel's visit before she had become pregnant and the visit to Elizabeth?

Luke tells us no details about the visit. But after the ceremony, when the family started the return journey to Nazareth, they found He was missing. They must have been distraught. They rushed back, they searched, and finding Him in the temple they rebuked Him! They rebuked Him! The Son of God rebuked! But how lovely it is to see that their relationship was so full and (dare we say it) so ordinary. He was learning by the things he suffered!

The doctors of the law had been amazed at His learning—at His perception. But it is the answer Jesus gave His distraught parents that stands out: 'I must be about My Father's business.' And it is perhaps appropriate that after this statement by Jesus, the next event recorded is his baptism!

Baptism: Jesus commenced His public work with baptism. What did this mean in his case? John the Baptist baptised men as a sign of repentance and cleansing and a determination to live a more godly life. In the case of Jesus, was this baptism something more than what would have been inconsistent with his holiness and his purity? Some have suggested that Jesus was baptised 'just in case there had been some inadvertent error in His past'. This is unthinkable! It would contradict His deity, and so we must reject any such suggestion. On the other hand, it is often suggested that He went through the ceremony simply to identify with men, but surely identification with sinners in baptism would imply deceit.

John the Baptist saw the obvious inconsistency in the request of Jesus, and at first he refused to baptise Jesus (Matt. 3: 14). Jesus, however, explained to John that His baptism would symbolise His own death and resurrection: ' In this way—by my death and resurrection—I shall fulfil all righteousness.'

Jesus had come to fulfil the law by living a perfect life, totally pleasing to His Father; and in his death he offered up to his Father the perfect sacrifice. By His death, it became possible for His perfection to be counted as mine and His righteousness to be imputed to me so that 'in Him' I am counted righteous by a holy God. This required His death (His death is counted as mine), and it required His resurrection (His life becomes mine), both symbolised in His baptism.

Baptism symbolises death, burial, and resurrection. In his own baptism, Jesus *looked forward* to His death, burial, and resurrection. In adult baptism, the symbol *looks back* to His death and resurrection and symbolises our involvement 'in Him'. The death of Christ is therefore central; and Christian baptism goes far further than the simple repentance, cleansing, and reformation of John's baptism.

THE TEMPTATION

3

The temptation of Jesus is a profound mystery. It is unthinkable that He could have sinned. Yet, if not, were the temptations real? Some resolution of this may be given by the fact that Jesus, while fully God (Col. 2: 9, NIV), faced temptation and overcame, drawing only on the resources that are available to each of us.

Jesus is about to enter into public service. This is marked by two events. First, His baptism: a demonstration as to how He would accomplish His mission by death, burial, and resurrection. The second, His temptation: a demonstration of His perfection and therefore His suitability for his mission. In addition, and most encouragingly for us, His overcoming of temptation was an example to us because He used only resources that are available to us. Also—and again, most encouraging for us—His temptation was part of His preparation to be our high priest; and because of it, we can pray for help to One who understands because He was here and was tempted in every point as we are (Heb. 2: 17,18; 4: 15,16).

Following His baptism, the voice of His Father's approval still ringing in His ears, Jesus must have been elated. Most of us are especially vulnerable to temptation when on a 'high', and we are inclined to be overconfident and reliant on self. Jesus was also in a very weak state physically from prolonged hunger. It is therefore helpful to compare the state of the first Adam, when Satan confronted him, with the

14

state of Jesus, 'the last Adam'. Both were sinless; both were in total communion with God the Father. Adam, however, was in a place of perfection and total satisfaction. Jesus was in a desert, with the wild beasts, weakened by a desperate hunger.

The temptations are well known: 'Make these stones bread', 'Cast yourself down from a high place on the Temple', and 'Fall down and worship me'. How real were these temptations to Jesus, and is there a common theme running through them? One of the commentators has suggested that in each of the temptations, Satan was saying to Jesus, 'Don't pursue the hard road you have chosen! What's the point? The people will never listen. All they want is peace and plenty, so give them bread. Or give them a really dramatic sign of your power?' (Edersheim says the Jews had a saying that when Messiah came, he would appear on the pinnacle of the temple. 'Go one better,' Satan appears to have been saying. 'Appear, and then cast yourself down!') Or why not take the greatest shortcut of all to a kingdom: 'Fall down, worship me, and I'll give you a kingdom!'

These were not the only temptations the Lord faced. Hebrews 4:15 states that He was tempted in all points just as we are. We can therefore come to Him with confidence: He will help us. He knows and understands what we face not just because He is God but because He was here and He faced every difficulty we face. So let us draw strength from our risen Jesus when we face temptation.

But also, let us learn from the way Jesus answered the temptations. The only resource He used was scripture. This is important not just because scripture holds the answer to every problem and to every difficulty we meet but also because it shows that the mind of Jesus was filled with scripture.

If an evil thought comes into our mind, there is no point trying to put it away and empty our mind. Psychologists tell us that one just cannot empty the mind. Just try to think about nothing! The only way to deal with undesirable thoughts is to displace them with others; and if we are regularly exposing our mind to scripture, there will be little room for evil thoughts in the first place. And when evil thoughts do occur, we can deliberately turn our thinking to something good and profitable. (What was that verse I read this morning before I left home?) Hence, Philippians 4: 8: fill your mind with things that are true, pure, of good report, etc.

Another most encouraging thought is to realise that whatever difficulty we face, it is common to man; and there is always a way of escape (1 Cor. 10: 13; 1 Pet. 5: 8,9). Never imagine that you are special in any way. Many others have faced the difficulties you face, and they have won through. Let that be an encouragement to you. And never be tempted to excuse yourself if you do give in: 'Well, no one could have withstood that temptation. Others would certainly have given in too,' Not so! Jesus (and other) have triumphed over Satan using only the resources that are available to you and to me!

The story is told of a man living in a dreadful environment who became a Christian. He was visited later by the person who had led him to Christ. 'How is it? How are things going?' the visitor asked anxiously. 'Well', the man said, 'it is as if there are two dogs in my mind. One is good and one is bad, and they keep fighting, fighting, and fighting all the time.' The person who had led him to Christ was puzzled. He had never heard such a description and felt it was somehow rather unscriptural. Hardly knowing how to respond, he blurted out, 'And which dog is winning?' 'Whichever one I feed,' came the answer.

4

JESUS CALLS MEN TO FOLLOW HIM (I)

Clearly John had been deeply impressed by his first meeting with Jesus. Sixty years later he wrote about it; and he was able to recall tiny details: the days of the week, the places, what Jesus had said, how men had answered. It had all been unforgettable. So it is with most men when they meet Jesus.

John starts his gospel record with a short account of the witness of John the Baptist (John 1: 26,27, NIV), and he records what must be one of the most 'electric' statements in the whole Bible: 'Behold the Lamb of God who bears away the sins of the world.' John the Baptist was what every true preacher should be: a pointer to Jesus, 'the Word', the communication from God. John caught the wonder of the phrase 'the Lamb of God' because he used it twenty-nine times in his later book, Revelation. The name is worth studying. Many of the Jewish sacrifices were of lambs, and so it will have been full of meaning to the Jews.

John the Baptist told two of his disciples to follow Jesus (35–37), and he then faded out of the story. As he had said earlier, 'I must decrease but He must increase.' The two men followed Jesus, and Jesus turned and asked them the most important question in life: 'What are you looking for?' (38). They spent the rest of that day and the next three years with Jesus. Clearly they found what they had been looking for, and they have been with Him ever since!

In reply to Jesus, the two men asked Him a question, 'Where dwellest thou?' A stupendous question! Imagine asking the Creator of all, the One whom the heavens cannot contain, where He dwells! Nevertheless, Jesus spent that night with them and many more just as He does with all those who seek Him sincerely. John was so deeply impressed that when he wrote about it 60 years later, he recorded the very time of the conversation 'about ten o'clock' (v. 39). John could probably even have pointed to the spot on the road where Christ had apprehended him. A man will never forget a meeting with Jesus Christ!

Peter too was changed by his meeting with Jesus, and he was given a new name to mark the occasion (from Simon [*hearing*] to Peter [*rock*]). The text indicates that Andrew had had to persuade Peter and had had to 'lead him on' to Jesus. If others are to be brought to Jesus, it may be necessary to lead them on into the truth about the Saviour.

Peter was not, of course, changed instantly by being given his new name. It was rather as if Jesus was saying, 'Simon, you are aimless and you have no purpose in life. Follow Me, and together, as you learn of Me, you will change and become a rock in a fickle, selfish, and evil world.' Jesus knows the full potential of a man; and in following Him and in serving Him, Jesus gives a man something to live up to, a goal worth striving towards.

Andrew is a lovely character. He is mentioned three times in John's gospel, and each time he is bringing someone to Jesus. In this chapter, it is his brother (41), later it is a lad with some bread and fish (6.8,9) and then some Greeks (12.22 NIV). A follower of Jesus will want to lead others to the Saviour.

Philip was an evangelist right from the start! He found Nathaniel and told Him, 'We have found the Christ.' Here is the secret of being a Christian. Christianity is not a mere philosophy. It is the following of a person. Christianity is a life—following Jesus, serving Him, and getting to know Him better day by day, situation by situation.

Perhaps the tiny account of the call of Nathaniel is the most remarkable of all. Nat was meditating when Andrew told him about Jesus. Verses 50 and 51 imply that he was thinking about Jacob at the time. The Lord knew this; and so when Andrew came to Him, Jesus greeted him, 'An Israelite in whom there is no guile.' What a testimonial this was from Jesus. But this was far more than just a cheery greeting by Jesus.

Israel had been the new name given to Jacob, and Jacob had been a man full of guile and deceit. Again, however, just as with Peter, Jesus is giving Nathaniel a name to live up to, a character to strive for, 'Israel' meaning a prince with God!

Jesus called twelve men to follow Him. Why? Couldn't He have gone it alone? Several reasons are given, but perhaps the most stimulating is 'He chose twelve to be with Him' (Mark 3: 14). Companionship is basic in marriage, in family, and in every other relationship. The basis of true companionship is communication and sharing.

Jesus was able later to say to His disciples, 'I have made you my friends for I have told you everything.' He invites His followers to share everything with Him. And this principle for true friendship applies in human relationships: Is our partner our best friend in this way? Do we really share and communicate with him/her? Do we show, by sharing, that we really value his/her friendship and companionship?

5

JESUS CALLS MEN TO FOLLOW HIM (II)

There is no difficulty in reconciling the call of Peter in John 1 and in Luke 5 NIV. John tells of Peter's first meeting with Jesus. It was some time before Jesus called him to leave everything and follow him.

Jesus has commenced his public ministry. He has preached in the synagogues in Galilee. Sadly, when He had spoken in His home church in Nazareth, the people had become angry at His claims and had tried to kill Him. Jesus never returned to Nazareth. They had had their, chance and they had thrown it away. In fact, they tried to throw Jesus himself away (see Luke 4: 29)!

Jesus is Lord of our work: Luke then describes how Jesus had been teaching by the lake side. A crowd gathers; and so that He will be heard, Jesus gets into one of the fishing boats moored alongside and asks the owner to row a little out from the shore. The boat is Peter's, and he remains in it with Jesus. Peter had been out fishing all night. He is tired, yet the teaching of Jesus captivates him!

As soon as He has finished teaching, Jesus tells Peter to start fishing again. Imagine Peter's reaction. He had had a fruitless night's fishing, and now a carpenter was telling him how to do his job! But the response of Peter is memorable: 'Lord, I'll do it because You tell me to.' In effect: 'Lord, I'll do it for You!' (5).

In every activity, motivation is crucial, and this is especially true in work. Why do we work? All too often, it is for selfish aims. Of course, money is important, but it should never be our sole aim. The response of Peter to Jesus gives the highest motivation for work: 'Lord, I'm doing it for You!' For the Christian, motivation in everything he does should be 'This is for You, Lord.' That may be hard, and it may seem unreasonable if the boss is a rogue. Yet scripture states that even slaves should do their work 'with all their heart . . . as they are working for the Lord, and not for men', and this passage goes on to promise an eternal reward for everything that is done for the Lord' (Col. 3: 22–25, NIV). Paul underlines all this: 'Remember—it is the Lord Christ you are serving!' Serving Christ will transform the bench and the kitchen sink!

It makes sense however we look at it. Whatever we do will die with us if it has been done only for selfish or trivial reasons or for purely materialistic aims, and at the final judgement all our 'wood hay and stubble' will be burnt up (1 Cor. 3: 12, NIV). On the other hand, whatever we do for the Lord will be of relevance throughout all eternity. Of course, there are some things about which we could never say, 'This is for the Lord.' But surely that gives us a basis for a fine test of our activities. If I cannot say I am doing something for the Lord, then perhaps I shouldn't be doing it at all!

There is yet another aspect to this. When Peter brought Jesus into his job, he learnt further aspects of His Lordship, and his former selfish motivation immediately seemed substandard and unworthy (see Luke 5: 8). Bringing Jesus into things will always enrich and never spoil unless, of course, the thing is wrong in the first place.

Jesus is Lord of our possessions: We are not told much about the call of Matthew, except that he left everything to follow Jesus, and his first act as a disciple was to declare his allegiance to Jesus publicly at a banquet!

Tax collectors were very wealthy men, and it must have been very costly for Matthew to follow Jesus. But let's remember that apart from Matthew, who gave up everything, there was only one man was told by Jesus to give everything away (Luke 18: 25, NIV). This may be necessary if we have a problem with money and material things. But to most of us, Jesus says, 'You are a steward of what you possess. Use everything you have, money and possessions, for Me, and for others.' Money has enormous potential for either good or bad; and again, as with work, a good moral test is to say, 'Am I using this for the Lord?' If we cannot say yes, then either we have too limited a view of His Lordship in our lives, or we shouldn't be using our money or possessions for that particular purpose.

Remember that just as God gave you your brain and your brawn, and you can use them in His service, in the same way, you can use all your money and possessions in His service—and you are accountable to God for both!

Don't dismiss any of this as sentimental idealism. On the one hand, every activity will be enormously enriched if we bring the Lord into it whether it is work or play. But also, everything we possess will gain an eternal significance, and we will enjoy it far more if it is dedicated to Him and used in His service.

Perhaps one of the most stimulating and challenging verses on this is Luke 16: 9 (NIV): 'Use money and possessions to make friends, so that when these things have passed away, you will have friends in heaven.'

6

THE MIRACLES OF JESUS

(Luke 5: 18, NIV)

Augustine asked, 'What is the feeding of the 5,000 compared with the patient process by which fields of wheat shoot up, bud and mature, and was used to make the slices of bread . . . over which you forgot to say grace this morning?' In fact, Scripture does not always sharply distinguish between the providence of God 'upholding all things' day by day and His special 'miraculous' acts. After all, 'God is in all things'. It is, however, the 'special acts' that most would call miracles, and a possible definition of them is 'manifestations of divine power of moral of spiritual significance'. This puts an emphasis on the why and not the how of the event.

At the same time, this definition equally well describes all the work of God: the balance and harmony of nature, as well as its original creation. This very point made by Paul in Romans 1: 20 (NIV) when he argues that 'visible' things are not just an evidence of His existence but also carries a spiritual message about God's character. That is, they fulfil the definition of a miracle.

What follows in this study are comments on the 'special acts' of God. What is said is not intended to be controversial, but sadly there are few subjects more likely to lead to controversy.

Three words are used for miracle in the original: *powers*, *wonders*, and *signs*. Each of these emphasises one aspect of the event. The most informative term, however, is *sign*. This is the word used by John throughout his gospel, and it emphasises that there is always a lesson to be learned from the event (see John 20: 30,31).

Miracles are not scattered throughout scripture. They are confined to periods when God was giving a new revelation. This is most important. For example, all but five of the fifty miracles in the Old Testament occurred either around the Exodus or during the time of Elijah and Elisha when the prophetic method of communication by God was at its height. New Testament miracles occurred when Jesus was on earth giving a fresh revelation of God and when the church, God's new society, was being founded.

Undoubtedly, the *purpose* of miracles is the most important issue by a long way, and how one sees the purpose will affect one's attitude to the miracles of scripture and to the claims made by some about miracles today. It seems that the basic purpose in virtually every miracle in scripture is to *give authority to the messenger and his message*. This purpose is in keeping with the definition given above.

A key passage is the incident in Luke 5: 18. A paralysed man is brought by his friends to Jesus. When Jesus saw their faith, He said, 'Your sins are forgiven.' Understandably, this cut no ice with the people standing around, so Jesus added, 'So that you may know that I have power to forgive sins, take up your bed and walk.' That is, anyone could make a claim to forgive sins because in the nature of that situation there can be no evidence here and now of forgiveness; and the statement made by Jesus, taken on its own, could have had no authority with the people. But the evidence Jesus then gave, in making a paralysed man walk, gave immediate authority to Jesus and to His statement about forgiveness. In the same way, Paul and others refer to the resurrection of Christ as evidence that gives authority to claims made in scripture about life after death, the final judgement, etc.

This purpose of miracles, the investing of the messenger and his message with authority, is evident throughout the record of the life of Jesus. For example, Jesus claimed that He alone can give lasting satisfaction in life, and so He called Himself 'the true Bread', who came down from heaven to give life to the world ((John 6).

This claim could have been (and is) dismissed by many as nothing more than wishful thinking, but the fact that Jesus had just fed 5,000 and more people with five loaves and two fish gave very powerful authority to His claims about Himself. If He can perform such a physical act, then let us consider His other claims very seriously! One aspect of miracles that follows from this purpose is that the miracles in scripture were primarily (though not exclusively) given to convince unbelievers.

Now before any judgement is made about present-day claims of miracles, let several things be said. First, God is sovereign; and of course He could do miracles today. Therefore, to question claims about miracles today is not to challenge the sovereignty of God but only to question the assessment by mere men.

Second, if someone is convinced that God intervened in a particular situation in a way that is meaningful to them, then may God bless that experience to them, but don't let them expect others to see the situation in the same way or to have the same meaning for them. Paul had a most mysterious experience, which he describes as 'having been caught up to the third heaven' (2 Cor. 12). It was intensely meaningful to him. Yet he mentions it only once in the context of a warning to the Corinthian church, and this was the most unbalanced church in the New Testament!

Paul mentions his experience with great reluctance, and he says repeatedly that he will not glorify in it. It might be advisable if those who make claims today treated their experiences in the same low-key, personal way as Paul did.

Then third (and with special reference to the claims today of miraculous healings), one cannot but question the competence of most of the people who make claims about miracles to judge whether or not something 'extraordinary' or 'supernatural' has happened. In particular, the diagnosis of disease is often exceedingly difficult, and even skilled specialists with every diagnostic facility can get it wrong. Furthermore, there are numerous cases recorded in the general medical literature of fatal diseases that have spontaneously regressed and disappeared.

But again, let it be repeated: God is sovereign, and no way should we appear to wish to limit His work. At the same time, while scripture warns us not to quench the Spirit, we are told in the same passage to 'test all things' (1 Thess. 5: 19,21). What is urged in what has been written above is not that we should question the power or the sovereignty of God but that we have every reason to question the judgement of men.

Jesus said, 'Believe me . . . or at least believe on the evidence of the miracles' (John 14: 11, NIV).

Belief, faith, and trust are difficult concepts. And yet they are simply natural human responses to evidence. David Hume (1711–76) pointed out that 'a wise man proportions his belief to the strength of the evidence'. In any situation requiring a decision, I have to base my belief and my response in terms of actions on whatever evidence I have relating to that situation. If the decision I have to make involves a friend or a contact, what I know about that person constitutes evidence upon which I have to base my decision and my action. If I feel that the evidence I have is inadequate, or something makes me doubt its validity, I will make enquiries to gain further evidence.

Jesus presented evidence about himself and evidence relevant to his message: his wisdom, the purity of his life, his insight into the heart of things, his handling of men. He seems to have believed that this should have been enough for men to accept the claims he made about himself—claims that in the nature of things were not directly testable. But He knew how men think and act, and so he gave further evidence in terms of miraculous deeds. And referring to these, he said, 'Believe me . . . or at least believe on the evidence of the miracles' (John 14: 11, NIV).

Two points are clearly implied by this statement. First, the miracles were not ends in themselves. Secondly, while the miracles involved purely physical things, the evidence they gave carried implications beyond the material. In fact, he made this last pretty clear by linking, in his teaching, the giving of physical sight with spiritual insight, the giving of bread with bread with spiritual satisfaction, and the clearest example of all in Luke 5: 20–24.

Belief, faith, and trust are difficult concepts. And yet life would be impossible without them. Every decision I take and every action I make is based on evidence; and in almost every situation, the evidence is limited and often of no direct relevance. I apply my reason to that evidence; and if still doubtful, I seek more evidence. I then make my decision, in faith, and my faith takes me beyond the evidence.

A model of the human response to evidence is as follows:

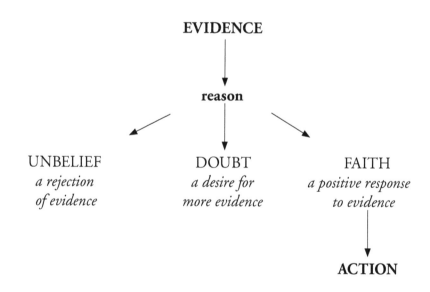

This same model can be applied to the response to spiritual evidences:

EVIDENCE

Creation. Conscience. The words and the work of Jesus,
His death and resurrection, the Bible,
the changed lives of believers, etc.

reason

The wisdom that comes from God (James 3: 17)
and the influence of the Holy Spirit within every man (John 16: 8–11)

UNBELIEF	DOUBT	FAITH
the rejection	*a desire for*	*a positive response*
of evidence	*more evidence*	*to evidence*
Matthew 28: 11–15	Matthew 11: 1–5	Matthew 9: 5–8
John 9: 34	Acts 17: 11	John 9: 36–38

ACTION

obedience to God

a consequence of
faith Romans 14: 9

a demonstration of
faith 1 John 2: 3

faith and works are
interdependent
James 2: 22–26

CHRIST: THE LIGHT
OF THE WORLD

(John 9, NIV)

Jesus made many claims relating to His origin and His nature, and many promises relating to our relationship to Him now as Saviour and Lord, and, later, to Him as our Judge. He gave evidence relating to all these. We can either respond in faith or in unbelief.

The authorities had just tried to kill Jesus by stoning (8:59); and as He leaves the temple, Jesus saw a beggar, blind from birth. He had compassion on the man; and despite the recent threat to His life, Jesus stopped. He had earlier claimed to be 'the light of the world' (8:12), and He now repeats this claim (9:5). He immediately goes on to give evidence by giving the man sight.

Now this miracle of Jesus was physical, and so it was not of direct relevance to His claim to be 'the light of the world'. Of course, there was no way that He could give evidence of that, but the miracle He performed by giving sight is evidence on the basis of which a response can be made to His greater claim. If a man can restore sight, then let's examine whatever else he says very carefully!

But what does the claim of Jesus mean, and in what way is the miracle evidence that He is 'Light to the world'? In every language and culture, *light* implies knowledge and truth while darkness implies ignorance and error. Jesus claimed to bring light—in fact, to be light from outside the physical realm: knowledge of the spirit world, of the afterlife, of judgement, and of destinies. Natural man has no knowledge of these things. In fact, the Bible teaches that because of sin, man is in spiritual darkness; and without receiving light and life from Christ, he will go into eternal darkness. If a man, however, comes to Jesus, he will receive light and life from Jesus in salvation.

In chapter 12, John seems to have recorded the final public teaching of Jesus. He repeated the claim that He is light (v. 46), linking this to both a promise and a warning. He says, 'I have come a light into the world: everyone who believes in Me will not remain in darkness' (v. 46). 'If anyone rejects what I say, I don't judge him—but the words I have spoken will be the basis of his final judgement' (v. 48). Jesus here warns that each man will be judged by how he has responded to the light he has about Jesus ('the words I have spoken').

The way in which this principle will be of relevance in the final judgement of the pagan who has never heard about Jesus is not clear from scripture; but for me, it is a clear warning that because I have free and easy access to the Bible and to the words of Jesus, I am fully responsible for my own destiny.

And what about those who have had little or no evidence of Christianity? How will they be judged? Jesus seemed to have such in mind when he gave a warning to the residents in Capernaum and other towns where he had performed many miracles and given much teaching. It will be worse for you in the day of judgement, he said, than for Sodom; for if the evidence you have had had been given to Sodom, it would have remained until this day. 'And I tell you, it will be more tolerable for the land of Sodom in the day of judgement than for you' (Matt. 11: 20–24, NIV).

This seems to indicate several principles that will be basic in the final judgement. First, a man will be judged by the evidence he has had. (12: 47,48 says much the same.) Secondly, Jesus knows how a man would have responded if he had had better evidence. Thirdly, there will be degrees of judgement, and Jesus will take this last into account in his final judgement.

Perhaps the relevance of this to us is heightened enormously by the thought that at the final judgement some will plead that they had been given distorted evidence. Perhaps they had been put off by Christianity by the attitude of their local church or by the behaviour of a friend who had claimed to be a Christian. Paul seems to warn us about this (2 Cor. 3: 3, NIV).

Remember, he says, you are a 'letter of Christ' written by the Spirit of the living God. That 'letter' may be the only evidence about Christ that some will have; and if the message read in us is distorted by an unchristian attitude or behaviour, perhaps they too will 'rise up against us in the day of judgement' (Matt. 12: 41,42, NIV).

The model that was presented earlier has special relevance here:

EVIDENCE
In addition to His previous teaching and miracles, the Lord now gave
further evidence in His miracle of giving sight to a man blind from birth.
This is acknowledged to be pretty powerful evidence
of a divine intervention (vs. 32,33).

reason
The Jews, together at first with the neighbours
(8,9) doubt what has happened.
Therefore, not unreasonably, they explore other explanations (9,19).
The man, however, applies other reasoning (32,33).

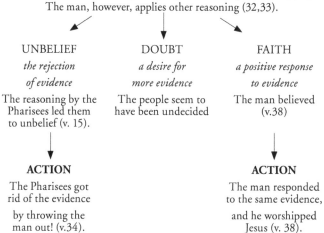

UNBELIEF	DOUBT	FAITH
the rejection of evidence	*a desire for more evidence*	*a positive response to evidence*
The reasoning by the Pharisees led them to unbelief (v. 15).	The people seem to have been undecided	The man believed (v.38)

ACTION		**ACTION**
The Pharisees got rid of the evidence		The man responded to the same evidence,
by throwing the man out! (v.34).		and he worshipped Jesus (v. 38).

CHRIST: THE
BREAD OF LIFE

(John 6, NIV)

Apart from the resurrection, the feeding of the 5,000 by Jesus is the only miracle recorded in the four gospels. All four writers saw it as being especially important for their readers. Jesus himself based many lessons on the miracle, and John takes 71 verses to summarise them all.

The account of the miracle is easily told. Crowds were attracted by the teaching of Jesus. Evening came, and he told the disciples to feed the crowd. They were astounded. 'Between us all we have only five small loaves and a few savoury fish!' Jesus, however, can use whatever is given to him; and so he took these, broke the loaves and distributed them together with the fish. He distributed them and distributed them and went on distributing them until everyone had had enough.

Picture the scene: Jesus calmly looking up to heaven giving thanks for the food, the crowd jostling to get their share, and the disciples watching Jesus with looks of utter incredulity. But just try to imagine the reaction of the disciples later. When all had eaten, Jesus told them to pick up all the leftovers 'that nothing be lost'! After all that abundance, he tells them to collect the scraps 'that nothing be lost'!

It has been pointed out that the basic purpose of the miracles is to give authority to the messenger and to his message. So it is here. Jesus wants to give teaching of such importance that it is recorded in all the gospel records. And evidently, there is something to be learned from the scraps!

Jesus claims that he is 'the Bread of Life' (v. 35). That is, he claims that knowing him, learning about him, and following him can sustain a man and satisfy his deepest longings throughout life and can meet his need at death in a way that nothing else can. Mark, in his account of this miracle, makes an interesting comment. He states that Jesus felt compassion for the crowds, 'for they were like sheep without a shepherd' (6: 34). They were not just hungry; they were lost and aimless. They had no purpose in life; they were just drifting along.

Of course, many religious leaders, politicians, and others have claimed that their teaching or their philosophy can satisfy. The trouble is that such claims can only be fully tested by following them throughout life to death itself. But Jesus gave evidence on the basis of which we can judge the likely validity of his claims. If a man can produce food miraculously and in abundance, then the other claims he makes about himself certainly deserve to be examined very carefully indeed!

The teaching of Jesus is difficult, and the demands he makes on his followers are certainly hard. Being a Christian doesn't make life easy, but it does make it incomparably worthwhile! In his teaching the day following the miracle, Jesus told his followers, 'To have eternal life you must eat my flesh and drink my blood, and if you do this, then you will abide in me and I will abide in you.'

That's hard—really hard to take. But of course Jesus was using language symbolically. He was speaking in pictures of the relationship a true Christian has with him. In the same kind of way the Bible says that a man and his wife become 'one flesh', meaning that their relationships is deep and full, and they are not to be separated from each other. So using the same kind of symbolism, Jesus says his relationship with a Christian is like 'eating and drinking' him and like 'abiding in him, and he in you'.

All this is hard and demanding. At the end of chapter 6, John records that when his followers heard Jesus say all this, many 'went back and followed him no more' (v. 66). It was too tough. Life is much simpler and easier back home, and in any case, can we be sure that following him will bring satisfaction? So Jesus turns to his disciples and asks them, 'Will you also go back?' And Peter, summing up the situation for them all, answered, 'Lord, to whom can we go? You have the words of eternal life' (John 6: 68, NIV).

In the end, Christianity is not a philosophy. It is not a way of life. It is the accepting of Jesus Christ for who he is and a total commitment to following him for life—and beyond. And the man who responds to Jesus Christ in this way has 'eternal life'. That is, he knows Jesus Christ, day by day transforming every aspect of life, guiding, and guilding every activity and every relationship and giving them an eternal significance.

But what about that strange instruction at the end of the feeding miracle: pick up all the leftovers 'that nothing be lost'? A strange instruction after a meal of plenty and after a demonstration that he could satisfy hunger. And what of the strange phrase 'that nothing be lost'? Is Jesus simply concerned about litter and the environment; or having performed a miracle on one day, is he apprehensive that he won't be able to provide for the disciples tomorrow?

Or is Jesus saying that nothing that we learn of him and no experience we have of him will ever be lost? This would seem to make sense of the final phrase in the Lord's instruction that nothing be lost. If this is his point, or one of them, it is certainly an encouragement to those who are ageing and are beginning to become forgetful. All that you have known of him, all you have experienced with him, all you have done for him, *nothing will be lost*. And as if to emphasise this, Jesus states that he himself will raise 'it' up at the last day. What an encouragement!

(On this last point, I have been given to understand that whereas Jesus says
'I will raise **him** up at the last day' in 40, he also
uses the neuter: 'I will raise *it* up' in 39.)

9

THE TRANSFIGURATION OF JESUS

(Luke 9, NIV)

The transfiguration of Jesus is one of the greatest mysteries in the life of Jesus. But this is precisely what we should expect. An interaction between the spiritual and the material will go beyond human understanding, and human language will be inadequate to describe it. However, we really should not ask, 'Why the transfiguration?'; but rather, He is fully God (Col. 2: 9), and so why was He not constantly in a state of transfigurement? The answer lies in that most interesting phrase: 'His flesh was a veil' (Heb. 10: 20). Just as the veil in the tabernacle and temple protected men from the glory of God revealed within the most holy place, so the flesh of Jesus protected men from the glory of Jesus.

Early in the gospels, the question is asked repeatedly: 'Who is this?' Herod asks, the authorities ask, the enemies of Jesus ask, and the crowds echo, 'Who is this?' Then Jesus Himself puts the question to the disciples, 'Whom do men say that I am?'; and before they can answer, He interrupts, 'And whom do you say that I am?' (Luke 9: 18–20, NIV). This is the most important question every man has to answer: 'Who is Jesus Christ?' Not who do others say he is? Ultimately the answer can never be second hand, and on the answer each man gives for himself will hang his eternal destiny.

Peter, spokesman for the disciples, answered the Lord's question, 'You are the Christ of God' (20). Jesus immediately began to explain to them that things would not be as they expected. He would be taken and would suffer and die (22). Peter was taken aback, and he rebuked the Lord for saying this. His concept of the work of the Messiah was clearly totally inadequate and misguided, and so the Lord had to silence him (Matt. 16: 22,23, NIV).

Jesus then seems to say to the disciples, 'Come up this mountain, and you will hear who I really am.' And on the mountain, the appearance of Jesus was altered. He became radiant, glistening; and His face shone as the sun; and then the vocabulary of the gospel writers seems to fail them. The spiritual began to interact with the material as He assumed something of the glory, which is eternally His. Two men appeared with Him, Moses and Elijah, the great lawgiver and the great prophet, both of whom had written of Christ. The disciples watched dumbstruck as these two spoke with Jesus.

Now if you met the Creator of the universe, what would you talk to Him about? What issues would you raise? Would you ask about the glories of heaven or about origins or destinies? Would you want to raise the problem of suffering? Or would you babble on like Peter?

In fact, the sole topic of interest to Moses and to Elijah seems to have been the death of Jesus. They discussed 'His death' (literally 'His exodus'), which He would accomplish in Jerusalem. Isn't that remarkable? Both Moses and Elijah had died centuries before and had already experienced something of the afterlife, and yet the burning issue for them was the death of Jesus. How astounded Peter must have been to hear this. A short time before, he had rebuked Jesus for talking about death, and here the two men whom Peter held in the greatest awe talk about nothing else!

Sadly the disciples were sleepy, and they seemed to have missed the whole conversation. Certainly, they recorded none of it. What a shame that none of it was recorded for us. Moses had led the exodus of Israel out of slavery and oppression in Egypt. Wouldn't it be marvellous to know how Jesus had explained to Moses the greater exodus He Himself would achieve for His followers, leading them out of guilt and judgement? But the disciples slept through it all!

And then a cloud covered the crowd on the mount of transfiguration. In scripture, clouds are usually associated with God's glory, and so it may have been that the personal glory of Jesus was absorbed into a larger glory; and out of this, God the Father spoke. He answered the question that had been asked by Herod, by the authorities, and by the crowds, 'This is My Beloved Son.' And then the voice added, 'Listen to Him.' There are so many voices; but ultimately, Jesus and only Jesus is the way, the truth, the life.

Peter was all for staying, but they had to leave the mountaintop. And so the eternal Son left the glory, as it were for the second time, and descended with His disciples into the valley of humiliation. There was a lad there who was distorted by sin and for whom men could do nothing (Luke 9: 40). Jesus gave the answer to his need and to the ultimate need of all men, 'Bring him to me' (41). Here is the gospel in a single statement: bring men to Jesus!

The Greek for *transfigure* gives us the word *metamorphosis*, and this is used to describe the change from caterpillar to butterfly. The word is used in only two places in the Bible: once for Christ and once with reference to us in Romans 12: 2 (NIV): 'Don't conform to the pattern of this world but be transformed by the renewing of your mind.' Don't try to be like men around you; rather, be changed from within by the daily adjustment of your mind and attitudes by modelling these on Christ. Or as Romans 13: 14 (NIV) says, 'Put on the Lord Jesus Christ and do not respond to your lower nature or think about how the desires of your sinful nature can be satisfied.'

10

THE MASTER'S MEN

Against a background of deepening confusion and growing opposition, Jesus trains His little band of disciples. He seeks to deepen their conviction as to who He is and lead them into a deeper commitment to Himself. Although they are a most unlikely collection of insignificant men, under His tuition, they are later charged with turning the world upside down!

Jesus called the disciples to follow Him so that He would have friendship and companionship. Mark put it that He chose twelve men 'to be with Him' (Mark 3: 14, NIV). That is a marvellous starting point for those of us who would follow Jesus. But Jesus wanted His followers to be active in His service. John therefore records His statement that the twelve had been chosen to be fruitful (John 15: 16, NIV). Is it not incredible that the Sovereign Lord chooses us as His companions and through us He will work out His eternal purposes? Add to that the fact that what we do for Him is of eternal significance. ('Your fruit will remain' [John 15: 16, NIV]).' All this invests us and what we do for Jesus with incredible value and dignity!

In Luke 9–10 there is a remarkable sequence of lessons about discipleship. One event after another taught the disciples either about Jesus or about themselves and their service—or about both.

* **Jesus sent His disciples out:** Followers of Jesus are not to withdraw. They are to go into the world, into society (9: 2).

We are not just to sit in our churches and expect people to come to us.

* **They met a hungry crowd**: Jesus challenged the disciples and said, 'Give them bread' (9: 13). John records that Jesus went on to explain that He is 'the True Bread that came down from heaven to give life to the world'. In the end, only Jesus can satisfy our deepest longings and desires.

* **Following Jesus is costly:** The Lord teaches that those who follow Him must 'take up their cross' and follow Him closely (9: 23–27, NIV). He also gave a warning to those who might be ashamed of Him.

* **The central issue in discipleship!** Jesus had asked the disciples, 'Whom do you say that I am?' On the mountain, they had seen Him transfigured and glorified, and they had heard God the Father declare who He is (35). The faithfulness of our following and the effectiveness of what we do for him will depend ultimately on how convinced we are about who Jesus really is.

* **Followers have limitations:** The disciples meet a lad who was in desperate need, but they have to admit that they could do nothing (9: 40). Jesus gives them a profound lesson: 'Bring him to Me' (41). We don't have many answers, but Jesus has, and he himself is the ultimate answer to man's needs.

* **Followers must be humble:** Perhaps there had been a bit of 'one-upmanship' amongst the disciples when they had been confronted by the lad who had needed help so desperately (40). Jesus took a child, set him in the middle, and gave the disciples a lesson on humility (47,48).

* **There is no place for arrogance in the Master's team:** Following Jesus makes some men proud and arrogant! John saw someone doing a good work, but he stopped him. Later, he told Jesus what he had done and added the complaint that 'he was not

following *us*! (49,50). Later, two of the disciples complained about the inhospitality of the locals and offered to call down fire from heaven on the villages! Luke records that Jesus rebuked them—one of the very few times that Jesus actually told his followers off!

* **Priorities have to be sorted out:** One who would follow Jesus must sort out priorities. What is the real underlying motive for my Christianity? If I am truly following Jesus, then He will be first and everything else will be in second place. After gently dealing with a few failures, Jesus said, 'Anyone who puts his hand to the plough and turns back is useless in the kingdom of heaven' (62).

* **You're not His only follower!** Jesus has lots of others who follow Him faithfully and serve Him effectively (10: 1). Elsewhere we are warned these are His servants and not ours, and I have no authority over them; however much I may disagree with them or their what they do (Rom. 10, NIV).

* **Joy and fulfilment lie not in success but in a relationship with Jesus:** The disciples returned to Jesus elated with success (17). Jesus didn't dismiss what they had done, but He told them the source of true joy: a relationship with Him. This gives security to us and to what we do and ultimately is the only relationship that can give total security.

Rejoice that your name is written in heaven. (10: 20)

Note: Books have been written on this topic (e.g. *The Master's Men, The Training of the Twelve*). One author points out that Jesus taught His disciples both by precept and by example. Listening and observing by the disciples taught them:

1. Lessons about Christ Himself:

    * His deity (the miracles/ the transfiguration)
    * His atoning work in His death and resurrection
    * The need for loyalty and devotion to Himself

2. Lessons about their own needs:

- humility (Luke 10: 46–48, etc.)
- forgiveness (Matt. 18: 21–35, etc.)
- prayer (Matt. 18: 1–14, etc.)
- tolerance (Mark 9: 38–41, etc.)

3. Lessons about their relationship with Him

- He called them servants, then friends, then brothers (see John 15: 15, John 20: 17, and Heb. 2: 11).
- He said that by His Spirit He would indwell them 14: 23).

4. Lessons about the world:

- its need (Matt. 9: 37,38, etc.)
- their responsibility (Matt. 38 leading to 10: 1, etc.)
- the attitude of the world to them (Matt. 10: 16–23, etc.)

11

OPPOSITION TO JESUS

(Matt. 12, NIV)

While the ordinary people listened to Jesus gladly (Mark 12: 37), the leaders of the Jews, who had much to lose in position and power, became increasingly jealous and showed a growing hatred. It is useful to consider the opposition to Jesus at a number of levels. In chapter 12, Matthew brings together a number of incidents, which illustrate this.

1. Natural but prejudiced objections: Jesus had a fresh approach to things. He was totally obedient to scripture, but He had little time for tradition. The leaders of the Jews put immense importance on their 'tradition of the elders', and so there was a continuing basis for controversy with any teacher of new things such as the way that Jesus ate with unwashed hands, His taking the place of a rabbi (an accredited teacher), and so on. He also upset many people by eating with 'tax gathers and sinners' and by not fasting (Mark 2: 16,18, NIV).

In chapter 12, Matthew tells how the Pharisees were upset when Jesus allowed His disciples to pluck ears of corn and eat them. All this represented work, which the scriptures forbade on the Sabbath. Jesus recognised this objection as sincere, and so He took time to carefully argue the point. He referred to an action by David and a practice of the priests in the Temple, both of which technically broke the Sabbath. Then He gently rebuked the objectors by referring to mercy as the underlying principle of the law and warned them that 'the Lord of the Sabbath' was amongst them. All this was said gently, and it gave them something to think about!

2. Prepared traps: While the Lord was always ready to discuss matters with an objector who was sincere, He reacted rather more sharply to those who were not genuine in their comments. Thus, when the Pharisees handed Him a coin and asked a loaded question, He gave an answer that was not just brilliant but also packed a punch! (see Matt. 22: 15–22, NIV). The same kind of response was given to questions about divorce, remarriage, the resurrection, etc., all of which were loaded and insincere (Matt. 22: 23–46, especially v. 15).

In chapter 12, Matthew tells how a man with a paralysed hand was used by his enemies to spring a trap (vs. 10–13). They set this man outside the synagogue (on a Sabbath!) and watched the Lord 'that they might find an accusation against Him' (Luke 6: 7, NIV). Jesus saw what they were up to, and He challenged them. No gentle explanations this time. They were utterly insincere, so He challenged them and then healed the man.

This is an interesting miracle. It might be thought that the Lord fell into another trap in that, just as the Pharisees were using the man, so the Lord used him in order to score a point against His opponents. Not so! The text states that following the Lord's command to the man, 'Stretch forth your hand', the man was healed 'as he stretched it forth'. In other words, the man responded to the Saviour in faith; and by responding, he received healing.

3. Plots to kill Him: On a previous occasion, his enemies had tried to kill Jesus. The first attempt had been right at the beginning of His public ministry (Luke 4: 29, NIV). The last attempt was, of course, within the purposes of God, and so it succeeded. In this chapter, however, Matthew records another attempt (12: 14). Following their humiliation by Jesus in His healing of the paralysed man, the Pharisees went out, called a council, and plotted how they might kill Him. And all on a Sabbath day!

4. False accusations: The enemies of Jesus did all they could to discredit His miracles. Once they tried to make out that a man who was claiming to have been given his sight by Jesus was an impostor (John 9: 19, NIV). A much more serious event is recorded by Matthew in this chapter (12: 22–30). After He had delivered a man from the power of a demon, the Pharisees claimed that Jesus had been able to do it only because He was in league with Satan (22–30). This was so serious a charge that the Lord did answer it and then proceeded to give His accusers a most serious warning (vs. 28,30). This kind of false charge is frequent today when the work of God is dismissed, for example, when the conversion of a man is dismissed as 'mere psychology'.

5. Demand for a sign: The leaders came to Jesus (Matt. 12: 38, NIV) and demanded a sign. Luke adds that their request was for a sign 'from heaven' (11: 16), implying that the miracles he had performed were not from heaven. Jesus clearly regarded this as a most serious implication because He gives an extended series of warnings (39–45). In fact, both the demand for a sign and the answer given by Jesus imply a rejection of evidence.

In effect, they said, 'These little miracles don't fool us. We are not just ignorant peasants. Give us a real sign—a sign from heaven!' Jesus warned them that the evidence a man has been given and the privileges he has had will be the basis for his judgement by Christ at the last day. This warning of Jesus is apt for today when so many casually dismiss evidence about Jesus.

6. Opposition from His family: It is strange that Matthew ends this chapter the way he does. And yet it is not so strange! Opposition from folk whom we love and respect is perhaps more hurtful and more discouraging than opposition from any other source. The new Christian expects his workmates or fellow students to rag him, but a few remarks from Mum or Dad or from one's partner can be devastating. Yet He is with us and in us. He knows and he understands because he experienced the same (Heb. 4: 15,16, NIV).

Matthew 12 is a remarkable chapter in bringing together these incidents of opposition to Jesus. The chapter is also remarkable for the statements about 'the unforgivable sin'. It is important that the warning of Jesus about sinning against the Holy Spirit is considered in its context. The event that immediately precedes this section (Matt. 12: 31,32, NIV) is the attributing by the Pharisees of the good, healing miracle of Jesus to a liaison with evil powers.

That was a most serious charge and represented a complete moral inversion on the part of the Pharisees. If a man calls good evil and evil good, his thinking is morally inverted and he is incapable of repentance. He is therefore unforgivable while in that state of mind. Furthermore, the Holy Spirit is 'the spirit of truth' 16: 13), and his work in the minds of men is to give conviction of right and wrong and of righteousness and judgement (John 16: 8–10). An inversion of right and wrong is therefore a sin against the Holy Spirit.

12

THE JOURNEY TO JERUSALEM

Luke seems give a central place in his gospel to the transfiguration.
The following structure has been suggested:

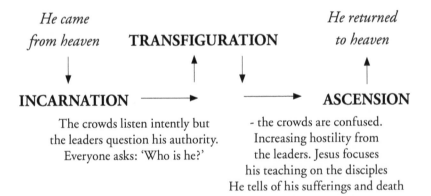

| He came | | He returned |
| from heaven | **TRANSFIGURATION** | to heaven |

INCARNATION ⟶ ⟶ **ASCENSION**

The crowds listen intently but the leaders question his authority. Everyone asks: 'Who is he?'

- the crowds are confused. Increasing hostility from the leaders. Jesus focuses his teaching on the disciples He tells of his sufferings and death

More than half of the Lord's public work is over. He has been several years on the road, demonstrating the nature and the qualities of God in human terms and in situations the common people could see and understand. He has explained about His kingdom of truth, of peace, and of love and the freedom and purpose in life, which membership of His kingdom can bring.

But none of this on its own is enough. He has to make it possible for men to be changed from within, to be cleansed and made fit for

His kingdom, and to come into an eternal relationship with Him and the Father. He Himself will have to provide the grounds for this to be possible, and this will require His sacrifice in death. So as if to re-commission Himself for the task, He briefly communes with the Father on the mountaintop; and then He sets Himself to go to Jerusalem to face rejection, suffering, and death.

Luke therefore seems to make a direct connection between the event of the demented boy on the day after the transfiguration (Luke 9: 37–42, NIV) and the transfiguration itself (28–36). The Lord is in glory on the mountain summit, communing with the Father (all of which could be taken to represent heaven). But He knows that down in the valley below, there is a demented boy, in the power of evil (representative of the kingdom of Satan), for whom nothing can be done (representative of man on his own). So Jesus leaves the glory, as it were for the second time; comes down to men; and calls the boy to Him for deliverance and freedom (all of which could be taken to represent His coming to earth in the incarnation).

Immediately after the incident with the demented boy, Jesus tells His followers about His coming rejection and arrest (Luke 9: 43–45, NIV), and almost immediately the journey to Jerusalem begins. As Luke puts it: 'The time came for Jesus to be received up and so He set His face to go to Jerusalem' (51). Luke 9: 51 is a watershed in this gospel, and Luke then treats the next ten chapters of a record of a single journey to Jerusalem.

This is consistent with Luke's objective, namely, to give prominence to the sacrifice of Christ and to show the purposefulness and determination of Jesus to accomplish the task, which had been given to Him by His Father and for which he had come to earth. So His course was set, His objective was clear, and 'He set His face to go to Jerusalem' (51). Furthermore, Jerusalem is stated to be the destination of that journey at least five times (9: 51, 13: 22, 17: 11, 18: 31, and 19: 28); and on three occasions He talked to the disciples about His sufferings and death, which would take place there.

It suited Luke's purpose to give this emphasis to the death of Jesus by portraying this journey to Jerusalem as a single journey. Yet we know from the other gospels that the journey took at least four months and that it had not been direct. In fact, John mentions two other visits to the capital for festivals.

The terms in which Luke writes about this journey to rejection, suffering, and death are remarkable. He went 'to be received up', and He went 'ascending to Jerusalem'. Of course, Jerusalem was on a hill, and so such terms might be literal, but there may be more than a hint of the excellence of the objective of that journey; and such a view would also be consistent with the way that John refers in his gospel to the suffering and death of Jesus as his being 'glorified'; and again, the word *glory* is used repeatedly by John when referring to his rejection, suffering, and death (e.g. John 12: 23 and 24, NIV).

On this last journey to Jerusalem, the whole situation seems to have changed totally from the situation of His earlier travels. The crowds are now confused, and their support is fickle, the authorities are openly hostile, and Jesus responds by teaching in parables. On the other hand, His concern for His followers is more intense; he talks more intimately to His disciples alone, He explains the parables, he tells them frequently about His coming suffering (Luke 9: 44, 17: 25, 18: 32, NIV) and at the end, He draws His disciples aside and gives them His highest and most sublime teaching in the seclusion of the upper room.

Note: In earlier years, many preachers dwelt on symbolism, and they saw 'types' and 'shadows' all over the scriptures. Some of it may seem now to have been contrived, but some were helpful. Symbolism can have the beauty and power of poetry. It is helpful to see the transfiguration presented as symbolic in the way outlined above. This has taken from Edersheim (*Life and Times of Jesus the Messiah*). That the gospel writers saw symbolism in the Lord's journey to Jerusalem seems to be indicated by some of the terms in which they described it: 'to be received up', 'He ascended to Jerusalem', and John's phrase, 'to be glorified'.

13

THE JEWISH FESTIVALS

Every Jew was obliged to attend three feasts each year, if at all possible: Passover, Pentecost, and Tabernacles. The value of these for us, together with the Jewish sacrifices, is that they all relate to the work of Jesus Christ. Study of them will therefore enrich our understanding and appreciation of His life and work.

PASSOVER: This is still the most important and basic festival for Jews. It reminded the people of their deliverance from slavery in Egypt and of their having become the people of God, travelling to a Promised Land. The central event was the slaying of the Passover lamb (Ex 12 NIV). This represented a sacrifice for their sins and gave protection from the angel of death. John the Baptist had cried, 'Behold the Lamb', pointing to Jesus, because He is our 'Passover' (1 Cor. 5: 7); and because of His sacrifice for sin, the judgement of God 'passes over' us.

Many details of the Passover sacrifice were fulfilled, item by item*, in the sufferings and death of Jesus; but the overall picture is that Jesus is our Saviour, and in Him we have deliverance from sin and from eternal separation from God, the penalty of sin. Paul, however, adds the warning that if He is our Passover, then we have been delivered from sin, and it is our responsibility to live lives of sincerity and truth (1 Cor. 5: 7,8, NIV).

* Exodus 12 lists many items of the Passover that were closely paralleled in the death of Christ. Thus, the tenth day of Nisan is probably Palm Sunday. The lamb was to be held for four days so that the family could ensure that it was blemish free and suitable for the sacrifice while Christ displayed his perfection openly during the last few days up to Good Friday. The lamb was to be perfect and in its prime as Jesus was from a human point of view. The lamb was to be slain 'between the evenings'—that is, at sundown—and it was then that Christ died.

One of the commentators states that the practice was to roast the lamb (roasting being indicative of intense suffering) on two spits, lashed together in the form of a cross. No bone of the lamb was to be broken. This last is remarkable in that John makes special mention of it in his account of the crucifixion. He tells that although the soldiers broke the legs of the two thieves, 'they brake not his legs' (John 19: 33, NIV); and then he quotes the command relating to the Passover lamb (37).

PENTECOST: Fifty days (*Pente-cost* in Greek) after Passover, the Jews were told to hold a feast of thanksgiving for the beginning of the harvest and they were to offer to God some of the very first harvest of their crops (Lev. 23: 15, NIV). This festival was fulfilled in the events related in Acts 2 'when the day of Pentecost was come' (v. 1), 'three thousand were converted to Christ' (v. 41). The first of the harvest of the gospel! Jesus fulfilled Passover,and His church received its first harvest at Pentecost when the Holy Spirit came.

Another aspect of Pentecost is that the Jews teach that their law was given at Pentecost (Exod. 19 and following). While Moses was receiving instruction from God on Mount Sinai, Aaron and the people set up a golden calf to worship. When Moses returned from God, he punished the people for their idolatry; and 3,000 died (Exod. 32). Paul, in 2 Corinthians (3: 7, etc.) contrasts the law, which brought death (3,000 died) and the Spirit, who brings life (3,000 received eternal life!).

TABERNACLES: This autumn festival celebrated the gathering of the final crops. It was a most joyful harvest festival. People attended a series of special thanksgiving services in the Temple, singing and waving palm branches.

Now the fascinating thing is that although the other festivals were fulfilled in the life and work of Jesus, this one was not; and John tells how Jesus refused to even attend this feast. When asked to go, He said to His disciples, 'My time has not yet come, but the timing is OK for you. So you go without Me' (John 7: 6, NIV). Strange words! But what Jesus was saying was 'You have no timetable for your life, but my life is all carefully planned, and it is not yet time for this particular festival to be fulfilled. Therefore, you go on ahead. I will come later.'

So when will this feast be fulfilled? The book of Revelation seems to give the clue. At the end of time, a huge crowd will gather in heaven drawn from every nation and tribe and language. They will stand before the Throne and before the Lamb of God, clothed in white, with palm branches in their hands, crying, 'Salvation to our God and to the Lamb upon the Throne' (Rev. 7: 9–17, NIV).

Of course, this is appropriate because a celebration to mark the completion of the work of the gospel and the final gathering into Christ's kingdom cannot be held until the end of time, and any hint of fulfilment by Christ would certainly have been appropriate.

At the same time, to go back to John 7, it is remarkable that Jesus did fulfil one part of the festival. While He carefully avoided going to the main ceremonies, He did make a surprise appearance at a little 'add on' ceremony, which took place each day of the festival*. Water was poured over a sacrifice in the temple, symbolising the blessing of God on the nation in the harvest.

Jesus seems to have chosen to join the crowds at the very moment this water was being poured on the final day of the festival, and He cried in a loud voice, 'If any man thirst, let him come to Me'. John, of course, gives a further deeper interpretation to the water being poured, speaking of it as the Holy Spirit (7: 39). This act of Jesus must have caused utter consternation, leading to controversy and a division among the people (43) followed by a bungled attempt by to arrest Him (44–53).

As with all the festivals and the sacrifices, there are many pictures of Christ and many messages for us in all this. This particular festival carries the warning that there is a time limit. The open invitation of the gospel will close one day. Another lesson arises from the 'add on' ceremony of the pouring of the water. If anyone thirsts for meaning, for purpose, for fulfilment, or for satisfaction, let him come to Jesus Christ. He will give him the Spirit, 'and from his innermost being will flow rivers of living water' (John 7: 37,38, NIV). My Jewish commentary ends its description of this festival: 'And you shall draw water in joy from the well of salvation.'

*There are various descriptions and interpretations of this ceremony, and they differ somewhat. The points made here have been taken from *The Jewish Festivals* by Rabbi Lehrman and from Edersheim's *Life and Times of Jesus the Messiah*.

14

THE GOOD SHEPHERD

(John 10, NIV)

The concept of Jesus as the good Shepherd is a treasured and most meaningful picture. He cares, tends, feeds, and protects those who follow Him; and for love of them, He laid down His life. The context of this chapter in John's record gives added impact to this picture. In chapter 8, John has related how the authorities had callously used a woman in an attempt to discredit Jesus. In chapter 9, those same authorities had attempted to discredit a man to whom Jesus had given sight, making him out to be an impostor; and after rebuking him sharply, they had thrown him out of the synagogue. Against this background, Jesus claims to be 'the good Shepherd'!

The idea of 'shepherding' is very prominent throughout scripture. The very first mention of God as shepherd was by Jacob. On his deathbed, Jacob referred to 'God, who shepherded me all my life long unto this day' (Gen. 48: 15, NIV). Isn't that encouraging for us? If God shepherded Jacob the deceiver, caring for him and protecting him and doing so 'all his life long', then surely I can expect no less.

David had had experiences that led him to develop the concept, and he wrote Psalm 23 in appreciation of shepherding by God. As a hymn, Psalm 23 is probably the best-known passage of scripture, and it is sung at almost every funeral. How sad it is when it is requested by relatives for the funeral service of someone who, in fact, knew nothing of the Lord as his or her shepherd. Still, it is probably the only hymn the deceased had known!

The idea of God as shepherd is prominent throughout the Old Testament. Ezekiel, for example, wrote at a time of great national distress; and he prophesied of a time when the Messiah would come and shepherding by God would be perfected: 'I will seek that which was lost. . . . I will save My flock. . . . I will set up one Shepherd. . . . I will make a covenant of peace' (34: 16–25).

In this same chapter, Ezekiel condemns the so-called shepherds of Israel at that time, 'Prophesy against the shepherds of Israel; woe to the shepherds that feed themselves, that have not strengthened, nor healed, nor bound up, nor brought again. . . . I am against these shepherds.'

Both these strands—condemnation of self-seeking shepherds and pastors and leaders and the perfection of the coming Messiah Shepherd—come together in the Lord Jesus Christ. Keeping both strands in mind will enrich our reading of John 10 and our experience of 'the Good Shepherd' in our own daily lives. Note that the word *good*, which describes our Shepherd here, is *kalos*, which means attractive, beautiful, winsome, as well as morally perfect.

Of course, many other prophecies of shepherding in the Old Testament found their fulfilment in the Lord Jesus. Zechariah prophesied that the coming Shepherd would suffer and die for His flock. 'Smite the Shepherd and the sheep will be scattered' (this part was quoted by Jesus Himself). 'And one shall say unto Him: "What are these wounds in your hands?" Then He shall answer: "Those with which I was wounded in the house of My friends"' (Zech. 13: 6,7, NIV).

Now read John 10. Doesn't all this background enrich enormously what Jesus says about Himself—His love and care for His flock (3,4,9); His laying down His life for the sheep (11,15) so that they might have eternal life (10); and His resurrection from the dead

(17,18)? 'He goes before His sheep' (4) is an especially meaningful phrase and not just in relation to death. Whatever difficulty or temptation we face, He has been before and He has fitted Himself to be our Shepherd by having exposed Himself to every situation we meet. We can pray therefore to a Shepherd: 'Who leads me through no darker rooms, than He has gone before' (Baxter).

Listening to these words as Jesus uttered them were some of those to whom the Lord would shortly delegate the task of shepherding His flock. Peter was one of these, and he in turn passed on the task to others. In his letter, Peter urged the leaders in the church to 'shepherd the flock of God among you, not under compulsion . . . and not for sordid gain . . . but with eagerness; nor yet as lording it over those allotted to your charge, but being examples to the flock' (1 Pet. 5: 3).

Peter had himself experienced the shepherding of Jesus; and perhaps with his own experiences on the night of his betrayal in mind, he refers in his letter the sheep that were going astray but are now returned to the Shepherd of souls (2: 25).

Early in these notes, the first mention of God as shepherd by Jacob was commented on. The last mention in the Bible is of equal interest. In Revelation 7: 17 (NIV), we are told that throughout eternity there will be no hunger or thirst anymore. Nor shall the sun beat down upon us, 'for the Lamb will be our Shepherd, and He will guide us to springs of eternal life'.

15

CHRIST IN THE HOME

(Luke 10, NIV)

Jesus honoured marriage, family, and the home in every way He possibly could. But more than that, He participated in the life and activities of the home. Marriage was not possible to Him, but He grew up in a normal home—and a poor one at that. He delayed the start of His public ministry so that He could act as head of a household, Joseph probably having died while He was young. All this meant that Jesus experienced every difficulty and every joy that we face in our families and in our homes. And so He fitted Himself for His role now as one who can be central in our homes and families.

The Lord visited two homes in Bethany. Simon, a man who had had leprosy and whom Jesus had probably healed, entertained Jesus to a meal. It had been a rather difficult occasion, with no real warmth (Luke 7: 36–50, NIV). Simon, the host, had omitted to show Jesus the common courtesies; and during the meal, a woman had caused quite an embarrassing distraction by weeping over Jesus and anointing His feet with ointment. Shortly after this, the Gadarene people had told Jesus to get out of their territory (Luke 8: 37, NIV); and Samaritan villagers had refused Him shelter (Luke 9: 52,53, NIV).

Against this background of rejection, and alongside the growing hostility of the authorities, the warmth and care of another home at

Bethany was outstanding. No wonder the Lord was a frequent visitor there, and no wonder he came to love that home.

It is explicitly stated that Jesus loved Mary and Martha, and Lazarus was referred to as one whom Jesus loved. It was probably one of the wealthier houses in the area, and some have suggested that Lazarus was the rich young ruler who had asked the Lord about eternal life (Mark 10). Others have suggested that Mary was the woman who had wept at the feet of Jesus in Simon's house. Whether or not these events are in the background, the Lord was warmly welcomed; and He was loved and cared for.

The picture of the home that emerges from scripture is beautiful and a model for us. The first mention is in Luke 10 after the harshness of Simon and the rejection of the Gadarenes and the Samaritans and shortly after all the activity of the evangelistic mission of the seventy disciples. Martha seems to have owned the house. She was probably the main homemaker of the three. She invited Jesus in (Luke 10: 38, NIV), and she seems to have been a most generous hostess.

Edersheim states that the Lord's visit was at the time of the Feast of Tabernacles. His disciples have gone ahead to the feast, and Jesus has no intention of going publicly to the celebrations until the end of the feast. So he visits Martha. Some have suggested that Martha may have been visited by some of the seventy (Luke 10: 1), and she may have expressed the wish to learn more. If so, the Lord responded to her invitation.

During the Feast of Tabernacles the Jews built booths, or shelters of leaves; and it may well have been in one of these that the Lord rested. Very soon after His arrival, the sisters sense His greatness and otherworldliness, and they respond, each in their own way. Mary becomes captivated and sits in rapt attention at His feet. Martha upgrades the meal and prepares an ever increasingly elaborate meal, with every little extra for her honoured guest.

Picture Martha, carrying backwards and forwards from the house to the booth, laying the table, setting out the best silver, arranging and rearranging. Mary, oblivious to what is going on, listening intently to Jesus. Eventually, Martha, 'distracted' with her work, bursts out in frustration to Jesus, 'Lord, don't you care that Mary has left me to serve alone?' She has 'left' me. Evidently Mary had started to help but had become captivated by the talk of the visitor.

How does the Lord deal with this delicate situation? First, note His gentleness: 'Martha, Martha'. The double use of the name was loving and gentle. It seems, however, that the Lord may have gently hinted to her that the meal she was preparing was unnecessarily elaborate. 'Martha, Martha, you are bothering about too many things. Only one dish is necessary.' (This is the translation of verse 41 by Weymouth and by Barclay).

Not that Jesus didn't value Martha's part. He certainly did. After all, it was her home and she had welcomed Him into it. It was simply that she had got things somewhat out of balance, and she had undervalued the part Mary had taken on. Let us learn from this little incident never to undervalue the part played by another Christian. If He is central, then He will value what is done—whatever balance we see!

The sisters were utterly different in their personality and their gifts. Martha, practical and sensible, attending to the material essentials. All essential but in balance. Mary, on the other hand, seems to have become almost instantaneously devoted to the Lord. Elsewhere, it is noted that she supported Jesus financially (Luke 8: 2, NIV). She was one of the few who remained at the foot of the cross. It was she who went early to the tomb, and she was the first to meet the risen Saviour. Clearly Mary came into a very special and loving relationship with Jesus.

There is need for both the Marys and the Marthas, and the Lord values the service of both. Jesus referred to the attention Mary gave Him as 'the good part', not *the better* part. Her communing with the Lord was not 'better' than the practical service of Martha. Both were necessary, and neither would be 'taken away'. The Lord was central in the thoughts of both, and He valued the service of both. So it should be in our homes and throughout our lives. Worship and practical service should both be evident, the balance being determined by how He has gifted us. Both are essential.

> *Lord of the pots and pans and things,*
> *Since I've no time to be*
> *A saint by doing lovely things,*
> *Or watching late with Thee*
> *Or dreaming in the dawnlight,*
> *Or storming heaven's gates,*
> *Make me a saint by getting meals*
> *And washing up the plates.*

There is yet another home that should be an encouragement to us. John wrote to a man called Gaius, who showed hospitality to strangers and 'sent them on their way in a manner worthy of God' (3 John 5,6, NIV). Bunyan had this character in mind when He described how Christiana, the wife of Christian, weary with travelling with her children, visited a house kept 'for the refreshment of pilgrims'. Gaius, the host, entertained any who passed that way, discussing scripture over the meal.

> *Now the hour was come when Christiana and her children must be gone, wherefore they called for a reckoning. But Gaius told them that at his house it was not the custom for pilgrims to pay for their entertainment. He looked for his pay from the Good Samaritan, who had promised that at His return whatsoever charge he had with them he would faithfully repay. Then they said to him: 'Gaius, you are acting faithfully in whatever you do for pilgrims, especially when they are strangers: and they bear witness to your love; and you do well to send them on their way in a manner worthy of God.'*

16

CHRIST: THE RESURRECTION AND THE LIFE

Jesus has just claimed that He gives eternal life to those who follow Him (John 10: 28, NIV). Faith is based on evidence, and so Jesus now proceeds to give evidence for His claim. The chapter is most important as it gives the highest evidence yet of the deity of Christ. It also shows the extremes of response by men to Christ. Some believe while others slip away to make trouble (46), yet another 'gem' in the chapter is the handling of the bereaved by the Lord.

In chapter 10 and elsewhere, Jesus argued that if a man would not accept His words, let him examine His works (10: 38). In other words, anyone can make claims. If we are to believe, let's have evidence! Hence, the use by John of the word *sign* in his record is significant. He uses this word rather than *miracle* (power or wonder) because the seven 'signs' he selected each gives direct evidence relating to a specific claim by Jesus.

Jesus had just claimed to be able to give eternal life to His followers (10: 28). He now raises from the dead a prominent, well-known man who had been dead four days in the presence of His enemies in a village adjacent to Jerusalem. All these points are important as no one could dismiss what he had done as rumour from distant Galilee. Those who doubted or dismissed His claims would now be challenged not just with His power but also with His deity. Hence, Jesus points out that what He does demonstrates both 'the glory of the Son of God' (v. 4) and the glory of God the Father' (40) at the same time—that is, an explicit claim to deity.

Notice that Jesus is the *resurrection* and the *life*. Is this mere repetition, or does 'life' take the idea of 'resurrection' further? Just as He rose on the third day, so at the end He will raise those who believe in Him (25). But they will not just be brought into some kind of meaningless, aimless existence; rather, they will experience the fullness and fulfilment of an eternal, ongoing, and developing relationship of life with God and with Jesus (see John 17: 3, NIV). On an earlier occasion, Jesus had made a most dramatic distinction between these and had underlined the difference by speaking of a resurrection to life and a resurrection to damnation (see 5: 21–29).

In addition to the central act, there are also a number of little scenes in this chapter, each of which is worth careful study. One is the Lord's handling of His disciples. As always, He seeks to strengthen their faith (see v. 15). The disciples are appalled by the proposal that they should respond to the message from Mary and Martha and go to Jerusalem (7). 'Lord, it will mean certain death!' warns Thomas.

Jesus answers by referring to the fact that light is limited to only 12 hours in a day (9). He has work to do, and the time available is limited. So it is for us. Let us walk (and work) for Him while there is opportunity, lest opportunities pass and darkness come upon us.

Light and darkness are major themes of John. Here, the disciples see going into Jerusalem as a journey into darkness and death. John presents Jesus repeatedly as the Light, who can deliver men from the darkness of ignorance and the eternal darkness of death. Following Him is therefore the only way to stay in the light even if it means going to Jerusalem or any other place of danger and uncertainty. Thomas gets the point: 'OK, let's go to Jerusalem *with Him* even if it means death!' (16). Thomas shows courage—no Doubting Thomas here—so long as Jesus is with them.

David had seen all this. 'Even though I walk through the valley, You will comfort me' (Ps. 23). That is, if we follow the Good Shepherd, He will give us strength to face dying and will lead us *through* death. (The O.E. word *comfort* is a transliteration of the Latin *con-forte*, which means *with strength*.)

Then the Lord comforts the two bereaved sisters, each in a different way. Martha had opened her home to Him; and because of this, her life and her home had been transformed. When she heard Jesus was approaching, she went out to meet Him (20). 'Lord, if only.' How often we say that in a difficulty or a crisis? Yet we seldom go on as Martha did: 'I know that even now whatever you ask, God will give you' (22).

Jesus replied with a remarkable statement, 'Your brother will rise', not 'He will rise' but 'Your Brother'. Surely, this implies that the relationships we make on earth will be preserved in the afterlife. An encouragement and a warning that is worth thinking about very carefully! The friends we make here will be our friends in eternity. Elsewhere, the Lord gave his followers encouragement to make friends for heaven (Luke 16: 9, NIV).

Jesus then deals with Mary. She had remained in the house until Martha had encouraged her with the most memorable words: 'The Master has come and is calling for you.' Mary goes to Jesus but is so overcome that she simply falls at His feet and weeps. Unlike Martha, Mary is too distraught to engage in a theological discussion, and so Jesus simply grieves and weeps with her (33,35). Here is Jesus 'learning through the things He experienced' in order to fit Himself to be our Great High Priest (Heb. 5:8 NIV). One day He will wipe away every tear (Rev. 7: 17, NIV) but not yet. Meantime, he encourages, strengthens, and even weeps alongside us.

The model of evidence and faith again has relevance here:

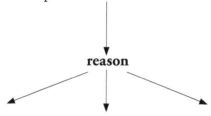

EVIDENCE
A man has been brought back to life
- rather powerful evidence of divinity

reason

UNBELIEF	DOUBT	FAITH
the rejection of evidence	*a desire for more evidence*	*a positive response to evidence*
The religious leaders	**The disciples**	**The people**
'See, this is getting us nowhere' so they made plans to kill Lazarus as well (10,19)	His disciples did not understand all this, only after Jesus had risen did they realise that these things had Been written about him (12.16)	Many people when they heard that he had given this miraculous sign, went out to meet him (12.18)

THE TRIUMPHAL ENTRY
INTO JERUSALEM

The end is drawing near. Opposition has been intensifying, and Jesus will shortly close His ministry with a final public appeal. Meanwhile, the people are confused. Some ask to see Him (John 12: 21, NIV), others demand to know who He is (John 12: 34, NIV), and the authorities plot His death. They also determine to put Lazarus to death because his testimony is leading many to faith in Christ (John 12: 10, NIV).

Jesus, knowing that the end is near, sends two of His disciples into a village to find a donkey upon which He will ride into the city. He had come to 'speak peace unto the heathen'; and so He enters the city humbly, on a lowly animal, rather than on a horse, which could have symbolised a conqueror. He instructs the disciples as to how they will find a donkey, and He tells them to explain to its owners that 'the Lord has need of it' or rather *'The Lord of it* has need' (literal translation of Luke 19: 31, NIV).

The owners of the animal were friends of Jesus, and He knew that they would acknowledge His Lordship over their possessions and would give their animal for His use. Jesus used that beast for His eternal purposes as He does with whatever we yield to Him as Lord. Material things are transformed when we acknowledge Him as Lord and ourselves as stewards.

As Jesus rode into Jerusalem, a huge crowd gathered around Him. Matthew, Mark, and Luke describe how the enthusiasm of the crowd practically swept Him into the city. John, on the other hand, describes how the people in Jerusalem, having heard all about the raising of Lazarus, went out to meet Him. Jerusalem in the early morning sun is a marvellous sight from the Mount of Olives; and yet, when Jesus saw it, He wept (lit. 'He wailed over it'). Luke describes this intense lament of the Lord (19: 41–45, NIV).

On entering the city, Jesus went straight to the Temple. He threw out all the crooked traders and rebuked them. Then the blind and the lame came to Him. He healed them and was immediately acknowledged to be the Son of David. Matthew, the most Jewish of the gospel writers, records this particular incident (21: 14,15, NIV).

Undoubtedly, Matthew had in mind the fact that when the city of Jerusalem had been first captured, the defenders of the city had mocked David by manning the defences with blind and lame men. David had cursed these; and after taking the city, he decreed that the blind and the lame were not to come into the Temple (2 Sam. 5: 7–9, NIV). Now that curse is reversed by David's greater Son as he invites the blind and the lame to come to Him in the temple for healing.

There are great difficulties in constructing a timetable for the days of Holy week, but the following is possible:

- **Saturday:** The Sabbath is spent in Bethany. After sundown, Mary anoints Jesus at supper.
- **Sunday:** The colt is fetched, and Jesus enters the city; He cleanses the Temple and leaves the city for the night.
- **Monday:** He teaches in the Temple, and the authorities challenge Him, 'By what authority are you doing these things?' He responds by challenging them and then warning them in parables (Matt. 21,22, NIV).
- **Tuesday:** The Jews attempt to trap Him with trick questions (Matt. 22: 15, NIV). He silences them (Matt. 22: 46, NIV) and goes on to condemn the scribes and Pharisees with eight 'woes' (more appropriately translated 'alas for you', showing

His concern even for those who opposed Him). The discourse on the Mount of Olives on the end times follows (Matt. 24 NIV). He tells the disciples about His betrayal and crucifixion. Judas goes to the authorities and 'covenants' to betray Him (Matt. 26: 14–16, NIV).

- **Wednesday:** This day seems to have been spent by the Lord in seclusion.
- **Thursday:** The first day of Passover (the Feast of Unleavened Bread). Peter and John are sent to prepare supper.

Why did the Lord spend these days in Jerusalem? Some have suggested that this was to fulfil the prophetic symbolism in the Passover lamb (Exod. 12, NIV). The Passover lambs had been the sacrifice by means of which the Israelites had escaped the judgement of the angel of death. And in order that each family would be assured of the purity of their Passover lamb and its suitability for sacrifice, the lambs had to be taken on the 10th of the month Nisan and kept until they were slain on the 14th Nisan. Keeping a lamb close would also enable each member of the family to get to know their lamb and therefore identify with it in its death.

So with Jesus. His triumphant entry into Jerusalem seems to have been on or around the 10th Nisan and His death on the 14th. His attitude and demeanour are utterly different during this week compared to that during His earlier ministry. Up to this time, His teaching had, on the whole, been quiet, appealing, and non-assertive. Repeatedly He had invited the people to come to Him; and when there had been opposition, He had moved on. In this final week, He challenges the authorities, He cleanses the Temple, He silences His critics, and He condemns the religious leaders.

And so Jesus gave further evidence of His purity, His moral perfection, and his excellence. And so He is *the Passover Lamb*, who has been sacrificed for us (1 Cor. 5: 7, NIV).

18

DIFFERENT RESPONSES TO JESUS

One of the key elements in the work of Jesus was His miracles (or 'signs'). These led some to respond positively and accept them as evidence relevant to the claims Jesus made for Himself. Others were confused. But standing apart were the authorities in Jerusalem who saw Jesus as an upstart who was fast becoming a dangerous rival. Some dismissed the miracles as having been done in Galilee, where the people were ignorant and naive. Others considered the miracles no more than clever tricks while yet others attributed them to the work of evil spirits. But then there was the raising of Lazarus from the dead!

The raising of Lazarus couldn't be dismissed. The miracle had been performed in a village next to Jerusalem. Lazarus had been well known in the city. He had been dead four days, and numerous people had witnessed his exit from the tomb.

Just try to imagine the situation. We tend to read the gospels unemotionally. Just try to imagine the situation. Suppose the one of our leaders died and after four days was brought back to life. The local interest would be incredible, the papers would be full of it, people from afar would come to see the man, a select committee of the House would be set up, and medical teams would apply for grant for research projects.

Now this is the background to the triumphal entry of Jesus into Jerusalem; and in the accounts of that event in the gospels, the raising of Lazarus is mentioned repeatedly. The main focus, however, is not on Lazarus but on Jesus: obtaining an ass, riding into the city, hearing the acclaim of the people, weeping of the Lord, and so on. But there are several references to Lazarus (see especially Jn 12:10,11 NIV), and none of these is incidental. Clearly, the raising of Lazarus was very much in the forefront of people's minds.

Put yourself in the place of one of those involved in these incidents. Try to give your imagination free play. How would you have reacted? How would you have responded to Jesus?

The villagers: Luke mentions a group of poor villagers (Luke 19: 31, NIV). Jesus sent to them and asked for their donkey. Put yourself in their shoes. 'I want your car', 'I need your house', 'There are some folk who need hospitality'. How would you have responded? How do you respond? At the request of Jesus, these villagers did not hesitate. They gave their donkey. The Lord needed it, so they gave it.

The disciples: The disciples didn't understand what was going on (John 12: 16, NIV). Put yourself in their shoes. Would you have understood? Would you have hung on, or would you have given up by this time and gone fishing? The disciples needed further evidence, and it was only after the resurrection of Jesus Himself that it all made sense. That is helpful to us. See everything in the life and work of Jesus in the light of His resurrection, and it will all come together. Without the resurrection, it doesn't add up.

The crowd: John records that the people 'were continually talking about Him' (see John 12: 17 in J B Phillips). Think yourself into the crowd. Join them as they flock out of the city, talking endlessly about Lazarus, 'It's Him, the one who brought that man back to life.'

The disabled: Matthew makes reference to some blind and lame people who came to Jesus (Matt. 21: 14, NIV). Why did they come? Jesus had just antagonised everyone in the Temple; and yet they came, limping and stumbling along, braving the Temple authorities. Why? Surely what they had heard about Lazarus gave them hope: 'If He could do that, surely He will be able to help us.'

The Greeks: John tells us that some Greeks came seeking Jesus (John 12: 21, NIV). In fact, the wording here implies that they sought an interview with Jesus! Imagine that! The philosophers and the logical thinkers asking for an interview! What a shame their interview with Jesus was not fully recorded for us!

The Pharisees: Undoubtedly the most remarkable group in all this drama was the authorities, represented by the Pharisees. Keep the other groups in mind—their excitement, their buzz, their enquiries and their interviews, with the whole city in flux—but the Pharisees stayed apart, plotting the death of Jesus! And even more incredible, they plotted to put Lazarus to death as well. Surely he had done nothing worthy of death. Yet he was proving to be a most powerful testimony to Jesus (John 12: 10,11, NIV). That's one way of handling evidence. If it doesn't suit your purpose, get rid of it!

Then, as now, there is a range of responses to Jesus from the acceptance of His Lordship to frank hostility. Possible responses include those who talk about Him, those who seek further evidence, and those who seek his answers to their problems. What is my response?

19

THE FINAL APPEAL
AND THE LAST
WARNING BY JESUS

(John 12: 35–50, NIV)

Light and darkness are prominent themes in John's record, and he uses the word light *more than twenty times. At the start of his record, John speaks of Jesus as 'the Light' that came into the world (3: 19), light that the darkness has never been able to extinguish (1: 4–9). Now, at the end of His public ministry, Jesus states that 'the Light' is going out of the world' (12: 35), and He warns that every man will be judged by his response to the light he has received (12: 48).*

We have followed Jesus through His teaching and His miracles in Galilee. He had made occasional visits to Jerusalem, usually at the time of one of the Jewish festivals. When he was there, there was always intense opposition. The authorities hated Him. They saw Him as an unlearned upstart who had not been taught in their rabbinical schools, one who had no respect for their traditions, and who represented a most serious challenge to their position and their authority. He was a dangerous rival, and yet the whole world was flocking to him (John 12: 19, NIV).

Now the end is approaching. Jesus wants to spend His last few days with His disciples, preparing them for His death and departure. So He takes His leave of the crowd and hides Himself (John 12: 36, NIV). He leaves them, however, with a final appeal and a warning, and these are as appropriate today as they ever were.

'You are going to have the light just a little while longer' (John 12: 35,36, NIV). Jesus came to give evidence about God, about the spirit world, about the eternal values. Many of us would like better evidence. A few statements and stories by a Man 2,000 years ago—is that all? Are we to commit our lives and trust for our future on that evidence alone?

Jesus warns that just as there are only 12 hours of light before the dark comes, so in the same way evidence is limited (John 11: 4,9, NIV). We cannot have all the daylight or all the evidence we might like. Neither can we have answers to all the questions we might ask. Yet the evidence presented in the Bible has been adequate for countless thousands who have committed their lives to Christ and even died for Him on the evidence in the Bible alone.

Who am I to demand better evidence? And if I do, what evidence would I ask for? Peter points out that the words of scripture are a surer source of evidence than any wonderful 'mountaintop' spiritual experience (2 Pet. 1: 16–19, NIV). An experience can, of course, be meaningful but only to the person directly involved and in the nature of things the memory of every experience fades and loses impact. On the other hand, scriptures can be consulted again and again and examined in the greatest detail.

Some had used just this kind of argument to Jesus. They had come to Him demanding 'a sign from heaven' (Matt. 12: 38–42, NIV). It was as if they were saying, 'These little miracles of yours, they may fool ignorant country labourers. We are educated. We are sophisticated. We deserve something better. Give us a sign from heaven.'

In answer, Jesus gave one of His most stern warnings. He called these men 'evil', and He warned them that one day many who had had far less evidence than they had would 'rise up in judgement against them'.

Jesus, however, did say that one further sign would be given: His own resurrection.

'Believe while you have the light, so that you will become "sons of light", otherwise darkness will overcome you' (12: 36). Jesus never promises that the Christian will be knowledgeable or will himself become a source of light. He uses the term *sons of light* to imply that those who believe in Jesus become related to 'the Light' Himself. I don't have many answers, but I know a man who does!

The alternative to knowing Jesus, on the other hand, is darkness; and the way Jesus phrased this is dramatic: 'Darkness will overcome you.' Without Jesus, a man has no guide, no principles and no purpose for this life, and no goal and no security for the future.

Then Jesus made a remarkable statement: *'As for the person who hears my words and does not keep them, I do not judge him. . . . the word that I have spoken will judge him at the last day'* (12: 46–48, NIV). That is, the basis for the judgement of each man will be the evidence he has had. The judgement of each man will therefore be reasonable and appropriate. No one will be able to object that his judgement is unfair: 'Shall not the Judge of all the earth do right?' This must be one of the most pregnant statements made by Jesus in relation to the final judgement and destinies. Hence, the final judgement will be worse for Capernaum, which was 'exalted unto heaven' by the presence and works of Jesus, than for Sodom, which had only had the witness of Lot (Matt. 11: 23, NIV).

Undoubtedly the most dramatic use by John of the contrast between light and darkness occurs in his description of the last appeal Jesus made to Judas. During supper with His disciples, Jesus gave Judas a titbit of food (the sop) as an offer of special friendship. With utter hypocrisy, Judas took it and then left the supper table to go and arrange to betray Jesus to the Jewish authorities. John states that Judas went out from supper, 'and it was night'. He walked away from 'the Light' *into eternal darkness.*

20

THE LAST SUPPER

(John 13, NIV)

One of the customs during the Passover celebration is for the youngest at the meal to ask the host, 'What is the meaning of this festival?' (see Exod. 12: 26, NIV). Presumably one of the disciples did ask Jesus, the host at the last supper, to explain the meaning of what they were doing. Alas, none of that divine commentary on the exodus was recorded for us.

The end was near, and Jesus was most anxious to have a last meal with His friends. He had much to tell them. There was some intensive teaching to be given; and He had to prepare them for His arrest, His sufferings, and death. The final events would be so traumatic and would come upon them so suddenly, and they were all so ill prepared.

So He arranged to have supper with them. But this would be no ordinary meal. It would be a Passover supper, the special meal that every Jewish family had each year to celebrate the deliverance of their forefathers 2,000 years before from slavery in Egypt and the beginnings of their nation as the people of God. How appropriate that meal would be. He Himself was about to become *the* Passover Lamb. His death would be the means of deliverance from sin; and within a relationship with Him, men and women could truly become the people of God. How appropriate the meal would be—a true Passover meal, a supper with communion between God with man.

So the arrangements were made. The Lord was filled with intense anticipation (Luke 22: 15, NIV), and the disciples nearly ruined it all! No sooner had they arrived than an angry row broke out about who should sit at the top of the table (Luke 22: 24, NIV). How could Jesus enjoy His last few hours with them in that atmosphere? And how could He commune with them and give them his highest teaching then when relationships were so strained?

How do you deal with this kind of situation? You sit down to an evening meal. You are tired, and all you want is a bit of peace and quiet, or you have something special to tell the family. And all the kids can do is squabble! You tear a strip off them, and how well they deserve it! But the atmosphere is ruined, and the rest of the meal is taken in silence.

Not so the Lord. He gently and lovingly shamed them into a better mood. He girded Himself with a towel, knelt before each of them, and washed their feet. 'Meekness and majesty, the Lord of eternity, kneels in humility and washes our feet. O, what a mystery!'

There was also the presence of Judas. How could Jesus talk about His covenant, which would be sealed by His own blood, when Judas had just been to the authorities? Judas too had entered into a covenant, an agreement to betray Jesus and to be paid for it (Luke 22: 5, NIV). How would you deal with an evil traitor who turned up at your supper table? Of course you would expose him and throw him out! He deserves no less! But how would that affect the atmosphere around the table?

Jesus, showing a love that is superhuman, invited Judas to be His friend. He reached across the table and offered Judas a choice morsel from the dish (John 13: 26, NIV). Judas deceptively accepted the loving gesture by Jesus, but His heart was set. So Jesus quietly gave him an excuse to leave the table, 'Judas, you have something to do. You can get on with it now.' The Lord's words were so gentle and quiet that the others didn't even realise what was going on (John 13: 28, 29, NIV).

Just as well. Had they known, there would have been an uproar. But then there followed the most ominous words in scripture: 'Judas went out . . . and it was night' Judas walked away from the Light into eternal night!

But just think about that situation. Satan had entered into the heart of Judas (John 13: 27, NIV); and so, at that supper table, the devil, incarnate in Judas, had been sitting opposite to God incarnate. It could not go on. Something had to give!

During the supper, Jesus showed a special concern about Peter. Peter was so full of himself at the meal that he would hardly listen (John 13: 36–38, NIV etc.). Jesus could easily have warned Peter not to go to the high priest's house because he would be unable to stand the questioning and he would deny all knowledge of Jesus. But had the Lord done that, Peter would have learnt nothing.

Peter was stubborn; and like many of us, he had to learn from his mistakes. He had to be allowed to go his own way. But over supper, Jesus insisted on having his full attention. 'Simon, Simon', Jesus said, and then He told Peter that He would pray him through the experiences of that night (Luke 22: 31–34, NIV).

Peter never forgot that night; and later, in his first letter, he referred to it repeatedly. Some of these references by Peter, writing perhaps 30 or more years later, are most moving. For example, he refers to a trial of faith being like the refining of gold; he speaks of 'returning unto the Shepherd of our souls', and he urges that we be ready with an answer for those who ask us a reason for the hope we have (1 Pet. 3: 15, NIV). Peter adds that we are to give our prepared answer in meekness!

In fact, the way Jesus handled Peter helps us to understand two phrases in the Lord's prayer. 'Lead us not into temptation', *but if we are unteachable, and you have to let us go into trouble, be with us and* 'deliver us from evil'.

Before Jesus commenced His intensive teaching, He had to prepare them for His betrayal by Judas. He knew that when the betrayal would happen, the disciples would be utterly shattered. Imagine their distress: 'He claimed to be God, and yet Judas fooled Him! How can He be divine? How can He be who He claims to be?' And so Jesus talked about the betrayal but only briefly so that they would not become distressed and so that the calm He had managed to restore to the evening would not be destroyed. And having told them briefly what was to happen, Jesus said a most important thing—something that indicates a basic principle in the handling of all prophecies in the Bible:

> I tell you now, before it happens, so that when it does happen, you will know that I AM. (John 13: 20, NIV)

Try to picture the disciples when Judas appeared later in the garden. Imagine the Lord being pointed out by Judas, the soldiers and Temple guards taking him, binding him, and leading him away. The disciples will have been shattered! But sooner or later, they will have remembered the words of Jesus, telling them beforehand, so that they would realise that he had known all along and that it was all within his divine and eternal purposes.

Do learn that verse, and think about it. It states a number of general principles in prophecy. It indicates the purpose for which prophecy is given (so that you will know). It indicates the time when a prophecy becomes relevant (when it happens), and it indicates the reassurance that it can give. 'I AM' is in control and is working out His purposes.

Prophecy is not given so that we can argue, divide friends, and split churches. Prophecy is given so that 'when it happens', we will be reassured and strengthened. The prophetic scriptures will become so very relevant at the end times. Those who know their Bible will see how the events have been foretold in scripture; and however terrible they are, they will demonstrate that God is working out His purposes.

In particular, the fulfilment of the prophetic passage will show that God is in control, that the I AM is operating and working out his purposes. And so, Jesus used the most appropriate name for Himself when warning the disciples about his betrayal. This is the name Yahweh, used in Exodus 3:14. God was about to deliver Israel, and He sent a message through Moses, 'I AM sovereign, I AM in control, I AM with you, and I AM about to deliver you.'

21

THE TEACHING OVER SUPPER

(John 13–17 NIV)

John has taken twelve chapters to record the three years of Christ's public ministry in Judea, in Samaria, and in Galilee. He now takes four chapters to relate some of the teachings of a single evening! This must tell us something of the importance of this teaching, often called the upper-room ministry.

The scene is set. Jesus knows that the time has come for His departure out of this world and back to the Father (John 13: 1, NIV). He now gives His highest teaching to those whom He loves. He has stilled their angry quarrel and has shamed them into a better mood. He has gently dismissed Judas. He has got Peter's attention and has given Him words that will sustain him later in his denial. He has gently prepared the eleven for their distress and disbelief when He is betrayed. They have taken communion together. He now settles down and opens His heart to them.

Notice the Lord's teaching method. First, notice the way that He states things in such a way that questions are drawn from His listeners. Not that it was a simple question-and-answer session—far more shrewd than that.

For example, in talking about His Father's house, He says, 'Where I am going you know, and you know the way' (John 14: 4, NIV). Thankfully, Thomas was there. He was a realist and was frank enough to say, 'No, we don't know where You are going, so how can we know the way?'

The Lord draws out questions like this several times (e.g. 14:8 and 14:22), but gradually His teaching becomes so sublime and exalted that the disciples listen in silent awe.

Secondly, notice the subjects upon which the Lord speaks are not kept apart but continually interweave and entangle together. One commentator calls this divine confusion. Teaching on the Holy Spirit is broken into five fragments, relationships with the world come up repeatedly, and so on. The Lord did not give a lecture, and these chapters are not lecture notes! Rather, the one who is *the Truth* is ministering to the needs of His friends, under intense emotion, and is appealing to their hearts as well as their minds.

Perhaps we should take note of this for our own study and for our teaching of others. There is a place for organised systematic lectures on Christian truth; but for most people, it is probably a relatively small place. Scripture is not written like Berkhoff's textbook of systematic theology. Rather, expository preaching that is true to the text will touch on a number of topics and will weave these together, indicating the relevance to everyday life, together with their practical consequences and their potential for encouragement.

In the end, effective preaching has to touch the heart and the mind and not just educate the listener! What a task, what a responsibility. No wonder James warns us about the responsibility of being a teacher as teachers will be judged by a very high standard (James 3:1).

It has already been noted that perhaps the most remarkable thing about these chapters is the focus of the mind of the Lord on that evening—His last evening. His whole attention is on the disciples. He was concerned for them all, with a special concern for Peter and for Judas. And once He had dealt lovingly and gently with Judas, the drama of the achieving of glory for the Son and for the Father commences (John 13: 31, 32, NIV). He well knew the purpose for which Judas had left the supper room, but now He turns His whole attention to the eleven, with no thought for what He Himself will shortly face.

Jesus returns repeatedly throughout the conversation to the fact that He will leave them. They are so ill prepared, and it is so hard to get them to listen, let alone understand. Leaving that aside, note that the first topic Jesus elaborates upon is their attitude and behaviour to one another. He Himself had just given a powerful demonstration of love. Now He applies the lesson he had just given: 'Love one another as I have loved you' (34).

Christian Love (Agapao): In Greek there are four words for *love* (Irish has eighteen!). Society—and, in particular, Greek society—had become so decadent that love was confused with lust, and as today every possible perversion was promoted. The most frequently used word was *eros*, which gives us the word *erotic*. Although scripture gives an exalted place to sexual love within marriage, this word *eros* is never used. To describe the love that should be shown by Christians, the New Testament writers coined a new word: *agapao*.

Vine's dictionary states, 'This distinctive Christian word can be known only from the actions it prompts. It is not the love of affection, nor is it drawn out by merits in its objective. It is not an impulse arising from feelings, it arises from the will and not feelings. It does not always run with the natural inclinations, nor does it spend itself only upon those with whom there is an affinity. It seeks the good and the welfare of others, it works no ill but seeks opportunity to do good to all men but especially those of the household of faith.'

In summary: Christian love is shown in the attitude it generates. Christian love is shown in the actions it prompts. Jesus gave us an example: *'As I have loved you'* (John 13: 34, NIV).

And then Jesus said a remarkable thing. He said that followers of His were to be distinctive and to be recognised by others not by the eloquence of their preaching, not by their different lifestyle, not by their holiness but by a love that would show in their attitude and in their deeds towards one another and towards others. And one is prompted to ask: if a stranger came into our church, what would strike him/her most? If someone met me, would he/she see anything distinctive, and if so, what?

22

THE WAY THE TRUTH
AND THE LIFE

(John 14: 6 NIV)

Jesus has begun to prepare the disciples for the terrible events that will suddenly burst upon them. He has already told them gently about the betrayal (13:21). Then He states that He will be with them only a little longer; and where He goes, they cannot come (13:33). Peter takes this up and questions Jesus. This leads Jesus to gently warn Peter about his denial (13:38), and Peter falls silent. These disturbing thoughts having been dealt with, Jesus calms the atmosphere again by saying, 'Don't be troubled—trust Me' (14:1).

The Lord was a superb teacher! Here, against a background of quarrelling followed by consternation and distress, the Lord leads the disciples along gently, restoring calm and gaining their rapt attention. Occasionally He makes a startling remark in order to provoke a question. He does this in chapter 14. 'Of course', He says, 'you know where I am going, and you know the way' (4). He does it again only a little later: 'And of course, you have seen God' (7). Both these statements wind the disciples up, they ask a question, and the discussion moves on.

We can be thankful that Thomas was present at the supper. Thomas, usually dismissed as 'the doubter', was a realist. There was nothing gullible about him; and while the others would let a thing pass, Thomas wanted to understand. So he speaks up here, 'Sorry, Lord, I don't have a clue, and if we don't know where you're going, how could we possibly know the way?' In reply, Jesus made one of His most memorable statements ever!

An utterly remarkable statement! Think about the phrases in his statement *'I am the way'* from one who would shortly hang on a cross, *'I am the truth'* when the lies of evil men would shortly triumph over Him, *'I am the life'*, and within a few hours He would lie in a tomb.

I AM THE WAY: Jesus did not say 'I am a way' or 'I am a pointer to the way'. In the original Greek, the *I* is emphatic, meaning *'I, I Myself, and I alone* am the way'. This is profound; and in these days of 'pleuralism' (the claim that there are many ways to God) and tolerance, it is widely unacceptable. There are, however, three levels at which we can consider Jesus as the Way.

First, if we are lost, we can follow someone who knows the destination to which we are going. Jesus is the Way in that sense. He came back from death and can give us reassurance about ultimate destinies. Then, if we want to meet someone, an intermediary can introduce us. Jesus is 'the Way' to God in that sense. But Jesus meant far more than either or both of these. The Christian message of salvation is all about forgiveness and cleansing and being IN CHRIST, clothed with His righteousness. The Christian is IN JESUS; and so He, Jesus himself, becomes, for the believer, the Way to holiness, to righteousness, to heaven, and to God:

> *Jesus, Thy blood and righteousness, my beauty are, my glorious dress.*
> *Midst flaming worlds, in these arrayed shall I lift up my head.*

I AM THE TRUTH: Jesus does not just claim that He is truthful. He was, and no one could accuse him of sin (John 8:46, NIV). Nor does He simply mean 'I reveal truth to you'. He did; and in his attitude and his behaviour, he shows us the character and the nature of God in human situations and in human relationships. As He goes on to say in verse 9, *'See Me—see God the Father!'* But more, far more, in Himself, Jesus is *the Truth*. In Him, in His purposes, lie the secrets of origins; in Him lie our destinies; and in Him are the answers to every question, every difficulty, every doubt we may ever express. He is in all things, and in him all things consist (Col 1:15–20 NIV)

I AM THE LIFE: This is perhaps the most profound part of the whole statement by Jesus. He is the origin and the creator of all things (John 1: 1–5, NIV). He alone is immortal (1 Tim. 6:16, NIV)—that is, all life is derived from Him. In Colossians 1 Paul states that in Him all things have their origin (v. 16); in Him everything is sustained (v. 17); in Him all things have their purpose; and in Him all things will, in the end, be wrapped up (v. 20). Perhaps, however, this phrase that He is the Life received its best explanation when Jesus gave a definition of eternal life:

> *This is life eternal: to know God and the One whom He has sent.*

A most important aspect of the statement by Jesus is that He did not make this statement with reference to heaven and the afterlife. He said it to a group of men who had growing apprehension about that evening and the next day and the next. And into that situation, Jesus said, 'I am the way to peace and security, I am the truth relevant to the difficulties and crises you will meet, and I am the life that will empower and sustain you and never leave you until I bring you to Myself at the end.'

> *Follow thou me. I am the way the truth and the life. Without the way there is no going; without the truth there is no knowing; without the life there is no living. I am the way thou must follow, the truth thou must believe, the life for which thou must hope. I am the inviolable way, the infallible truth, the never-ending life. I am the straightest way; the sovereign truth. life true, life blessed, life uncreated.* (Thomas à Kempis, *The Imitation of Christ*)

23

KEEPING HIS COMMANDS

(John 14: 15–26, NIV)

Jesus has just said, 'Ask whatever you like and I will do it' (14: 14). No, not quite! Jesus is not to be used or manipulated. The full statement Jesus made implies that there are very clear limitations and restraints on our asking. Jesus therefore said that requests are to be made 'in His name' and are to be 'for His glory'. Furthermore, requests are to arise within a relationship of love. All this excludes the casual or selfish request. And Jesus went on to state that the evidence of love for Him is the keeping of His commands (14: 15) and the obeying of His teaching. Within that relationship, ask whatever you like!

When we became Christians, we were brought into a relationship with God as His children. Jesus therefore called His disciples 'My little children' (13: 33), and He later reassured them that they would not become 'orphans' when He left them. But a relationship has to be developed. Just as in human relationships, so in spiritual relationships. A boy meets a girl, falls in love, and they marry. But all too often, a beautiful friendship ends in marriage!

Relationships, and especially marriage, have enormous potential; but it has to be worked at and developed. And just as many marriages just drift along without developing the togetherness, the shared interests, and the support and encouragement needed for full development of character and potential, so in just the same way many Christians drift along, developing little of the potential they have in their relationship with Christ.

A relationship between people implies a sharing together, and the extent to which aims and purposes are shared will determine the depth of a relationship. And the basis of a deep relationship is love; and for the Christian, this is not merely an emotion but an attitude of the will: the wishing of the very best for the other. The success of a marriage will be determined by the extent to which a couple share together, focusing on the desires and the needs of his/her partner and working for the happiness and fulfilment of the other partner—that is, the degree to which agapaeo is shown by each partner.

As in human relationships, so in spiritual relationships; and in these chapters, Jesus says a number of things about our relationship with Him and, as a consequence, our relationship with one another. He starts with love for himself, but he links this with obedience to him: 'If you love Me you will obey Me' (14: 15). There are two aspects to this.

First, the way we behave is an evidence of love. In fact, conduct is the only real evidence of love. Talk is cheap, and we can say wonderful things, but it is our actions that show whether or not we really love our partner. As in human relationships, so in spiritual relationships.

In fact, in this very chapter, there is the most powerful example of how actions demonstrate love. This is the only place where Jesus speaks directly of His love for the Father (31). He says, 'So that the world may know that I love the Father: as the Father has commanded me, so I do. Let's go,' and he went to the cross.

The evidence of His love is that He left the warmth and fellowship of the supper room and went out into the night to meet His betrayer and to go to his death. This incident may have been in John's mind when he later developed the theme of obedience as the evidence of His love and as a challenge to our behaviour (1 John 3: 16–18, NIV).

The second aspect of behaviour is that love should ideally be the sole motivation of everything we do. Let's be honest, however! If we wait until we are driven by love, or if we only do those things that are prompted by love, we will do little or nothing. Of course, love is the best motive, but don't be paralytic! Get on and do things!

The Ephesian church was told that it had lost its love, but it was not told to wait until its love had been rekindled. It was told to get on and 'do the first things' (Rev. 2: 4,5, NIV). In fact, love and service are interdependent, the one helping to promote the other. Just as love promotes service, so serving Christ and others will kindle love.

So what are His commands in verse 15? Is there a list of dos and don'ts for us to follow, like the blueprint used by a builder or engineer? Of course not. To see the marriage relationship in such a way would destroy it; and as in human relationships, so in spiritual relationships. Obeying a person is different to being obedient in an organisation or obeying a system. Obeying a person means acting in ways that will promote the best in the relationship and continuing behaviour in only such ways.

In fact, the connection between love and behaviour is common in John; and elsewhere, he links obedience with Christ's teaching and Christ's words. This takes the idea far beyond mere dos and don'ts to living in a way is consistent with the character and the nature of the one whom we love and follow.

Paul puts all this in another way. He does not give a set of dos and don'ts, but repeatedly he urges us to 'walk worthy'. We are to walk worthy of the Lord (Col. 1: 10, NIV), of God (1 Thess. 1: 12, NIV), and of your calling (Eph. 4: 1, NIV) so that you may be counted worthy of the kingdom (2 Thess. 1: 5, NIV). Doesn't all this dignify daily living as a Christian, and doesn't it give life as a Christian an eternal dimension? Elsewhere, Peter, writing to slaves, put it: 'You serve the Lord Christ.' Doesn't that elevate every activity in daily living?

Love, however, is a response to what we know about a person. As we get to know a friend or marriage partner, we love them more and more deeply; and this shows in our attitude and in our behaviour. Just as in human relationships, so in spiritual relationships. Our love for the Lord will grow as we get to know Him better from reading the scripture and in living out daily relationship into which He has brought us. Again, Paul has a neat way of putting it: 'Put on the Lord Jesus Christ,' and you will not gratify the desires of the sinful nature (Rom 13:14 NIV).

24

THE HOLY SPIRIT: THE SPIRIT OF TRUTH

(John 14: 16–18, 14 :26, 15: 26, 16: 8–15, NIV)

A good dwelling in Israel at the time of Jesus would have had three stories. The ground floor was the kataluma, *or shaking-down place where travellers dismounted, dusted themselves off, and untied their loads. When Jesus had been born, there had been no room—not even in the kataluma. The second floor was a reception room, the* pandocheion, *(literally 'all receive'). This is where the good Samaritan brought the wounded traveller. On the upper floor was the best and most private room: the* anogeon *(literally: 'above ground'). Jesus had instructed the disciples to ask for the kataluma, the humblest place for His last supper. But he said the good man will give you his best: a large furnished upper room.*

Supper is over. In the calm atmosphere He has created, the Lord talks and the disciples listen with rapt attention as His concern focuses upon them alone. He encourages them and prepares them for the future while He makes only passing mention of His own arrest, sufferings, and death. He speaks to them of love, joy, and peace; of relationships with Himself; of their attitude to others and to the world; of their security in Him; and of their fruit bearing. And all the time, He knew what was going on: Judas, the authorities, and the Roman soldiers!

This discourse is one of the main sources of teaching on the Holy Spirit, and on that we now focus. Jesus returns repeatedly to the work of the Holy Spirit after He has died, has been resurrected, and has left them. His Holy Spirit will indwell those who obey Him (14: 16–18), the Spirit will teach them (14: 26; 15, 26; 16: 11–15); He will reveal truth (14: 17, 14: 26, 16: 13) and will exalt Christ (16: 14–15); and He will convict men of sin, of their accountability, and of their final judgement (16: 8–11).

Notice two fundamental things about the Spirit of God. First, He is the *Holy* Spirit. Jesus explained that after His death the Spirit would come in a way that would be new: 'He will abide with you and shall be *in* you' (14: 17). The Spirit of God had been active throughout the whole period of the Old Testament. He had been 'with' men and had 'come upon men' who had been chosen for special tasks, principally those men who revealed God's will to the people in prophetic messages. But when He had died, Jesus explains, the cleansing of hearts and minds will be possible; and so the Holy Spirit will be able to *indwell* those who love him and follow him.

Secondly, the Holy Spirit does not promote Himself. His task is to exalt Christ. 'He shall not speak of Himself. He will glorify Me. He will take the things of Me and make them known to you' (16: 13,14). This should restrain what we expect of the Holy Spirit and what we say of Him. The church has undoubtedly neglected the Holy Spirit in its teaching, but that does not justify a focus upon Him or prayers to Him or songs to Him. We open ourselves to the Spirit when we promote Jesus Christ in teaching, in song, in prayer, and in worship.

There are a number of ways in which the teaching by Jesus about His Holy Spirit could be summarised. Perhaps one of the best is by dwelling on the names Jesus gave to Him or names implied by what Jesus said about Him.

The Indweller: While this is not strictly a name given to the Spirit, it summarises an essential truth about the Spirit. Jesus promised the Holy Spirit to the believer. Indeed, in Ephesians 1: 14, He is called the *arabon* of the believer, a word used in Greece for an engagement ring,

the commencement of an eternal relationship with infinite potential
for development. We should not therefore pray for the Holy Spirit.
He is in the believer, indwelling him/her. Rather, we should pray for
a greater sensitivity to Him, the Spirit. Paul's prayer for the Ephesian
Christians in Ephesians 1: 17,18 expresses this well.

The Teacher: The Holy Spirit exalts Christ. Before we read
scripture, we should pray for the help of the Holy Spirit in giving us
understanding; but then we should also pray for courage to live out
whatever He teaches us!

The Spirit of Truth: Clearly, this is linked to the above name. Jesus
had just called Himself *the* Truth (14: 6). He is the teacher about
Christ, He reveals truth, and the content of His teaching and His
revelation is Christ.

The Comforter: Literally the word is Paraclete, one called to one's
side. A very early translation coined the word *comforter*, derived
directly from the Latin *con-forte*, 'with strength'. If we appeal to the
Holy Spirit, He will give us strength to stand in a testing situation,
strength to overcome a difficulty, and strength to endure whatever
might bring us down. Jesus further promised that if a situation were
desperate, the Holy Spirit would have a special role (Matt 10:19 NIV).

Advocate (lit: one who speaks for us): Paul told the Roman
Christians something most encouraging about our praying. He said,
'We do not always know how to pray appropriately, but the Holy Spirit
within us prays for us in agonising longings for which we cannot
find adequate words, and God, who knows the secrets of our hearts
understands the intentions of the Spirit as He prays for those who love
Him' (Rom 8:26 NIV).

The Witness to the World: The Holy Spirit operates on the heart and
mind of every man so that every man has an innate knowledge of right
and wrong and a knowledge that in the end they are accountable, and
there is a final judgement (John 16: 8–11, NIV).

25

CHRIST'S LAST BEQUEST

(John 14: 27–29, NIV)

Jesus bequeathed His spirit to His Father. He gave His mother into the care of the beloved disciple. The soldiers took His clothes. Joseph of Arimathea was given His body. The one thing He gave to His disciples was His peace. 'Peace I leave with you, my peace I give unto you. Not as the world gives, give I unto you. Let not your heart be troubled neither let it be afraid. In the world you will have tribulation, but be of good cheer: I have overcome the world.'

Jesus knew all things. He knew that Judas had left the supper to make arrangements for the betrayal. He knew the soldiers were arranging His arrest. He knew that the Jewish authorities were plotting His death. He knew all this, and yet He talked to His disciples about peace! Peace in the midst of deceit and treachery, suffering, and death!

The peace Jesus gives is not achieved by withdrawal. Jesus sends His followers into the world 'as sheep amongst wolves'. They are to go *into* the world. They are to be salt and light *in* a dark and hostile society. No seclusion, no opting out, no withdrawal. And yet, in every situation, the follower of Jesus is to have peace. Not a superficial disregard or a careless attitude to difficulties. The peace a Christian can have is deep and stable. It arises from within. It is not vulnerable to mood or to circumstances. At the same time, it does not protect from trouble or difficulty.

The first and most basic level of the peace Jesus gives is 'peace with God'. As the old hymn, put it, 'It is well with my soul.' The Christian will never come into judgement. He has been forgiven. Christ has died for His sins. The Christian need not fear death. His destiny is secure. His relationship with God is eternal. Jesus, the Prince of Peace, has made 'a covenant of peace' with all those who come to Him for salvation.

The second aspect of the peace the follower of Jesus has is a basis for good relationships with those around him or her. Of course, this is experienced primarily with other Christians. Those who are 'in Christ' have unity, they share a common life in Him, and this should be apparent in the attitudes and in the behaviour of Christians to one another. But the peace of God should go further than just within the church. 'Pursue peace with all men,' Paul urges. Christ died for those around us, and we will answer one day for the attitude we show and the relationships we have established (Rom. 14: 19, NIV)

The third aspect is an inner peace. The Christian can be at peace with Himself. Whatever deficiencies and imbalances I feel I have, whatever my past has been, whatever mistakes I have made and sins I have done, there is forgiveness. The past is past. But more than that, I have been brought into an ongoing and developing relationship within which I have the assurance that I am loved and valued and within which I have been given a purpose.

He gave Himself for me—even for me! As Billy Bray, a street evangelist in Cornwall, used to shout, 'I'm the son of a King!' Even more than this! God has given me His Spirit, working within me, helping me to sort out my deficiencies and my imbalances. I awake every morning to a new day 'with Christ at my side'.

One of the most meaningful aspects of all this is that we can have peace in the face of unfairness and injustice. Some Christians experience cruel injustices and hurts, and the worst hurts are those that come from other Christians. These can lead to a consuming indignation and anger because the things were not in any way deserved. This anger can be exceedingly damaging, and the damage can be not just to a person's own circumstances but to his or her attitude and to his or her relationships. An imbalance can develop, a focusing on the hurt and perhaps on a desire for revenge. All this can be destructive and not to the one who originally caused the injustice or the hurt but to the victim himself or herself.

Jesus gives the potential for peace in such situations. Whatever has happened, the Christian can know that he or she is loved and valued; and however difficult the hurt is to bear, there is peace and utter security in the end. This can and should be very real whatever the situation. And yet there is more! Jesus left us an example, and we should follow in His steps.

No one was treated more unjustly that He. He did no wrong, yet He was falsely accused. He was reviled and scorned. He suffered and died 'for sins not His own'. Peter tells us that in all this, He left us an example that we should follow in His steps (1 Pet. 2: 21, NIV). He was able to bear it all meekly because 'He committed His cause to the One who judges rightly' (1 Pet. 2: 21–24, NIV).

Here is a marvellous defence for the Christian. When falsely accused, when unfairly treated, when hurt by things are not fair, we can take the matter to the cross and leave it there. One day it will be sorted out by the one who judges rightly: the God of recompenses. Justice will be done in the end. It may not be easy, but the Christian has an answer to personal hurt and injustice. He or she can take the matter to Jesus, leave it with him, and get on with life.

> These various aspects of peace can be summarised in three phrases: The Christian has *Peace with God* (Rom. 5: 1, NIV) because his sins are forgiven and Christ is His Saviour and Lord. He has the *Peace of God* (Phil. 4: 7, NIV), and this should flow out of the Christian into every relationship and should affect every activity. But this is not just a philosophy to be worked out as best we can on our own. The Christian has the very *God of Peace* dwelling within Him (Phil. 4: 9, NIV). Let us pray for a greater sensitivity to the God of Peace present within us by His Spirit.

26

PETER DENIES HIS LORD

'This is the true grace of God. Stand fast in it'. These are the concluding words of Peter in a letter, written as an old man, knowing that he was shortly to suffer a violent death. In fact, Peter states this as the reason for having written the letter (1 Pet. 5:12, NIV). What lies behind this statement?

During supper, Jesus had shown an acute concern for His disciples and a special concern for two of them. Although Peter was the most forward and the most confident of all the disciples, the Lord knew that he was buoyed up by Dutch courage. Shortly this would evaporate under questioning, and he would deny all knowledge of Jesus. However, the concern of the Lord was not that He Himself would be let down and denied by one of His friends. Rather, His concern focused entirely on Peter, on Peter's security, and on his faith.

On the arrest of Jesus, the disciples all forsook Him and fled. So much for the claims of loyalty they had all made during supper. Peter had gone further than any of them in assuring Jesus of his faithfulness even though these deny you, yet will not I. And fair enough, while the others had fled, Peter had followed the arresting party 'afar off' as they had returned to Jerusalem. He had even gone into the high priest's house and had stood with the guards and others around the fire in the courtyard. Matthew puts it that Peter 'wanted to see the end'; and while it is clear that this means the end of the matter of the arrest of

Jesus, one could be forgiven for thinking that Matthew means the end of Peter!

The night was cold, and Peter mingled with the soldiers and guards around the fire. But he was uneasy. He sat for a while (Luke), then he stood), and then he went to the porch (Mark). His unease drew the attention of others, and he was questioned about his knowledge of Jesus. Luke's record implies that from the fireside, Jesus could be seen as He was interrogated; and John tells how Jesus was asked closely about 'His disciples and about His doctrine' (John 18: 19, NIV). This may have prompted someone at the fire to prompt Peter to go the aid of Jesus, 'They are asking about his followers. Go on. You can help the man'. Peter denied all knowledge of Jesus, and after he had repeated the denial to Malchus, the cock crew, 'and Peter went out and wept bitterly' but not before the Lord had 'turned and looked upon Peter' (Luke 22: 61, NIV).

The look that Jesus gave Peter is not described, but it must have reminded Peter of the upper room and of the words with which Jesus had prepared him for this failure; but at the same time the look from the Lord must have been full of understanding, compassion, and forgiveness. As grief overwhelmed him. Peter must have had an underlying assurance that Jesus would pray for him and his faith would not fail.

> Simon, Simon, behold, Satan has desired to have you that he might sift you as wheat: but I have prayed for you, that your faith will not fail. And when you are turned, strengthen your brothers. (Luke 22: 31, 32, NIV)

Peter loved the Lord; and while Judas showed mere remorse and hanged himself, Peter repented and was forgiven by the Lord both in private (this may be implied in 1 Corinthians 15: 5, NIV) and later in public when he was restored to a position of trust as a shepherd of the Lord's sheep and lambs (John 21, NIV). God can use our failures for His glory and hence the charge Jesus gave to Peter in the upper room: 'When you are restored, strengthen your brothers.'

What an encouragement Peter must have been in the early church when many had to face torture and death under the Romans. But what will have been Peter's words of encouragement? They will certainly not have been 'Be like me: I stood alone!' Rather, he will have urged a dependence upon Jesus: 'His grace is utterly dependable, He prays for you; you are totally secure and your faith will never fail. Now stand fast in that assurance! This is the true grace of God. Stand fast in it' (1 Pet. 5: 12, NIV).

In the letter Peter wrote later, as an old man, there is yet another most challenging statement based upon Peter's experience on that night of denial. Peter wrote, 'Make Jesus Lord in your hearts and be ready to give a reasoned answer to anyone who asks you for the reason for the hope you have' (1 Pet. 3: 15, NIV). Again we can ask, what lies behind that statement?

At supper with Jesus, Peter had been the big man, the tough guy. Repeatedly he had assured Jesus of his loyalty: 'Though all men be offended because of you, yet I will never be offended' (Matt. 26: 33, NIV); 'Lord, I am ready to lay down my life for your sake' (John 13: 37, NIV); 'Lord, I am ready to go with you, both into prison and to death' (Luke 22: 33, NIV). Yet when the heat was on, it took only a remark from a maid for Peter to deny all knowledge of Jesus. But then, suddenly, the swearing and the denials turn to weeping! The weeping of a broken man who had denied the one whom he loved above all others.

And so Peter urges his readers: 'Make Jesus Lord.' Work out his lordship in your life, and think through your relationship with him so that when you are challenged, you will not be caught out and say something you will regret later. Rather, think things through and have a carefully thought-out answer ready.

27

JUDAS BETRAYS JESUS

The view that Judas was predestined in some way to betray Jesus and was not a free agent in the situation seems to be widely held. I think there are more important things to teach rather than challenge this view.

I believe this view to express a totally wrong understanding. In fact, I believe that to hold such a view makes the action of Jesus during supper, in offering Judas the sop, a cruel hypocrisy. Every commentator seems to agree that the sop was a morsel offered as a special mark of friendship. If Judas had been programmed to betray Him, then the action of Jesus would have been a cruel deceit. Rather, I am convinced that Jesus was utterly sincere, and his offer to Judas was genuine: 'Be my friend, Judas. You don't have to do it, but if you are determined, then there is no reason to wait.' Hence the remark in John: 'That thou doest, do quickly' (John 13: 27, NIV). This gave Judas a chance to leave without alarming the others and disturbing the tranquillity of the supper.

Morison, in *Who Moved the Stone?*, traces the likely movements of Judas after he had turned his back on 'the Light of the World' and had gone into the night. He probably went straight to the enemies of Jesus and offered to lead them to Jesus. Luke put it that the authorities covenanted with Judas to give him money (Luke 22: 5, NIV). This makes quite a contrast with the use of almost the same word by Jesus a few verses later in Luke's account: 'I covenant you a kingdom' (29).

Many hours, however, seem to have elapsed between the departure of Judas during supper and the arrest in the garden. A number of reasons have been suggested for the delay.

The Jewish authorities probably hesitated to arrest Jesus because their power to put a man to death was limited, and they feared the Romans too much to act illegally. So they probably went to Pilate and persuaded—or bribed—him into collusion. Procula, the wife of Pilate, whom tradition says was a secret disciple of Jesus, may have overheard some of their discussions and hence her warning to Pilate the next morning: 'Have nothing to do with that just man, for I have suffered many things this day in a dream because of him' (Matt. 27: 19, NIV).

Pilate, however, agreed to the arrest and presumable he agreed to follow things through the next morning and issue a death sentence. He therefore gave orders for some soldiers to accompany the Temple guards and arrest Jesus. Jews were not allowed to carry arms and hence the swords (Roman) and the staves in Luke 22:52 (NIV).

Judas probably led the party to the upper room where they made a noisy entrance but failed to find Jesus. Judas therefore led them to the Garden of Gethsemane, where he knew that Jesus had spent many a night (Luke 21: 37, NIV). Some believe that the upper room was in the home of Mark's mother; and it has been suggested that Mark, awakened by the arresting party, may have followed them to the garden. Mark may therefore be the young man mentioned in Mark 14: 51 (NIV).

How appropriate that Jesus went to the Garden of Gethsemane (the garden of the olive press). Olives were crushed and the oil used in sacrifices under the old covenant. We can only watch with the disciples from a distance as Jesus was crushed as He 'offered up prayers and supplications with strong crying and tears' (Heb. 5: 7, NIV). Then, His praying done, He is in full control and meets the arresting band with majestic calm: 'Heaven in His look and peace on His lips,' as one writer puts it. When challenged, the Lord simply said, 'I AM', again using the divine name from Exodus 3. His calmness and dignity were so totally unexpected that the arresting rabble stumbled and fell back in confusion. Was Judas transfixed by that 'I AM', leading John to comment that while the others fell about in confusion, Judas remained standing before the great I AM?

Many have tried to explain and some even to excuse the action of Judas. It could be that Judas was frustrated by the apparent hesitancy on the part of Jesus to seize power and deliver the Jewish people from the oppressive Roman rule and that he tried to precipitate Jesus into action. Even if this, or some other, is the explanation, it does not excuse Judas. His sin was not just that he covenanted with evil men or that he opened himself to the devil (Luke 22: 3–6, NIV). His greatest sin, and the one above all others for which he will be condemned, was that he rejected Christ and deliberately turned his back upon the Light. This will be the basis of the judgement of all men (see John 3: 18–20, 12: 46–48, NIV).

There are a number of gardens in scripture. It was in a garden that the first man rejected God, it was in the garden of the oil press (Gethsemane) that Christ took the cup of suffering, it was in a garden the triumph of His resurrection was announced, and it will be to paradise (literally, a garden) that He will take His redeemed followers.

28

THE TRIALS OF JESUS

The Lord went through a number of examinations during the night and the following morning. He was taken first to Annas and then to Caiphas. The Sanhedrin was then hastily gathered the next morning for a more proper but still irregular trial. He was then taken to Pilate, who sent Him to Herod, who returned him to Pilate for the death sentence.

The Lord endured mocking and inhuman treatment by the soldiers, including a flogging under which many a man died. He was shown no courtesy or kindness. He was allowed no sleep and given nothing to drink. His early death may have been due to dehydration in addition to blood loss and extreme physical exhaustion. He suffered dreadfully; and in this He fulfilled Isaiah 53, Psalm 22, and many other Old Testament prophetic passages.

At the same time, two things must be held in balance. First, scripture says very little about the physical sufferings of the Saviour; and what little is said is written with great dignity. We should therefore be very careful when speaking about these matters not to dwell on the physical or what is not in scripture. Secondly, the picture that comes over again and again is the Lord's deep concern for the destiny of others. We saw this in the upper room with Peter and with Judas, and here it is most noticeable that Jesus was concerned with the eternal destiny of Pilate rather than with His own defence; and at the end, his concern focused on a thief.

The Jewish trials: Ananias and Caiaphas are well known from contemporary Jewish writings. Cold, calculating, and cynical, they cared little for anything religious and manipulated things to their own financial advantage and that of their families. They are thought to have run the stalls within the Temple, which had been overturned by Jesus. They certainly will have wanted to get rid of this carpenter from Nazareth who had dared interfere in things in Jerusalem. Caiaphas had already stated so (John 11: 47–52, NIV).

No account of what happened before Annas is given. In all probability, Jesus remained silent. There was no sincerity in that man. The 'trial' before Caiaphas was more elaborate, with a semblance of justice. Being at night, however, it was still totally irregular under Jewish law. Witnesses were called, and the Lord invited to defend Himself.

Again, the whole thing was rigged, and the Lord remained silent— until He was put on oath by the high priest. This was a wrong thing to do, but the answer of the Lord led to the court losing every trace of legality in their treatment of their prisoner (Matt. 26: 62–68, NIV).

The Jews, however, could not carry out a death sentence, and so they had to involve the Roman governor. The collusion of Pilate had probably been arranged (or bought) the evening before. But notice the dreadful hypocrisy of the Jews recorded by John (18: 28, NIV). They wouldn't go into the residence of Pilate, a Gentile, lest they became ceremonially unclean and could not participate in the Passover feast. Yet they would put a man to death on a false verdict! Such is unredeemed human nature!

But notice that John does not dwell on this or on any other of the illegalities and indignities. The supreme purpose of scripture is to exalt Christ even in his sufferings and humiliation.

Jesus and Pilate: The Jewish leaders illustrate well the saying 'Power corrupts. Absolute power corrupts absolutely.' It was the same with Pilate, an obstinate and tactless man who ruthlessly forced his will on others. On at least three occasions, he had angered the Jews unnecessarily; and when they protested, he had put them down mercilessly (e.g. Luke 13: 1, NIV).

Yet in his examination of Jesus, we see a very different man. Why did a man, who shed innocent blood without hesitation, show such reluctance to sentence Jesus to death? Three times he declared Jesus innocent. He sent Him to Herod; in the episode with Barabbas, he had tried to release Jesus; and in the end, he attempted to absolve himself by washing his hands (Matt. 27: 24, NIV).

The explanation may well lie in the little incident with Procula, his wife (Matt. 27: 19, NIV). Tradition states that she was a secret follower of Jesus; and however bad a man is, a good woman can have a profound influence on him. No doubt too, the Holy Spirit was operating in the mind of Pilate exactly as the Lord had indicated (John 16: 8–11, NIV).

Perhaps the most dramatic scene in these chapters is when Jesus—scourged, humiliated, and crowned with thorns—stands before Pilate, in all his pomp and arrogance, representing the might of Rome, discussing power (John 18: 33–38, NIV). But it was love, not power, that held the Saviour there; and it was his concern for the soul of Pilate that led the Lord on in their discussion.

The way the Lord takes the questions of Pilate and leads on towards deeper issues is, to say the least, masterly. Jesus leaves aside questions as to His own state and speaks about truth: 'I bear witness to the truth. . . . Everyone that is of the truth listens to Me.' All this is clearly the Lord pleading with Pilate to discuss eternal things with Him. Sadly, although Pilate is challenged, he dismisses it all: 'What is truth?'

That same question 'What is truth?' is being asked today, and the answer usually given is no less dismissive than the answer given by Pilate, 'It all depends. What is true for you is not necessarily true for me. There are no absolutes.'

Lessons for us: Christ suffered alone, and no man has suffered like Him. Nor can we add anything to the redemptive sufferings and death of Jesus. His death alone is the grounds for our forgiveness and our reconciliation with God. We can add nothing. Jesus suffered 'alone' in every sense of that word.

And yet, a most remarkable thing is that scripture tells us that Christ, in His suffering, is to be the example that we should follow (1 Pet. 2: 21–25, NIV)! That is, if we are called on to suffer unjustly, we are to be like Him. Not that many of us will, in fact, suffer! Other than a bit of taunting and occasional embarrassment, most of us have a very soft time. But if we do meet opposition, if we do suffer unjustly, we are to take Christ as our example. We should 'follow in His steps', as Peter puts it. How can we possibly do this? How do we imitate Him?

Peter wrote to people who were suffering unjustly; and in drawing upon the example of Christ, he wrote:

> *When He was reviled, He reviled not again, when He suffered He threatened not, but He* 'committed His cause to the One who judges rightly. *(1 Pet. 2: 23, NIV)*

Therein lies the bottom line for us when our back is up against a wall. We don't have to struggle and protest and fight for justice. The Christian should maintain 'an eternal perspective'. God is a God of recompenses. The final verdict lies with Him, and that verdict will be fair and just! This should enable us to keep our cool, whatever the situation, however unfair things are!

In his description of the sufferings of the Messiah, Isaiah referred to Him as a sheep 'silent before its oppressors'. This certainly fits the behaviour of Jesus before the Jewish authorities. Jesus, however, used the same word with reference to His followers: 'Behold I send you forth as sheep in the midst of wolves.' He went on to tell how they would be betrayed and would be delivered up for trial (Matt. 10: 16–22, NIV).

In such a situation, Jesus encouraged His followers not to be anxious as to how they would answer their tormentors: 'Take no thought how or what you shall you shall speak, for it will be given you in that same hour. . . for the Holy Spirit will speak in you.' Some who have been tortured and been tried for the faith have told how this is true, how they were able to bear suffering greater than they had imagined and answer an interrogation more wisely than they would ever have expected.

Never let us think, however, that this promise of Jesus gives us an easy way out. Think your faith through, Peter urged.

> *Make Christ Lord, and be ready with an answer for those that ask a reason for the hope you have. But do this with gentleness and respect. (1 Pet. 3: 15, NIV)*

Peter himself had had no answer for those who questioned him about His following of Jesus. Nor was he given any answer by the Holy Spirit. Peter failed simply because he had not made Jesus Lord in his life and had not prepared a response. And remember, the word *answer* that Peter uses in the verse quoted above is 'a reasoned defence' (apologia) and never a slick answer. And that answer is to be given with gentleness and respect. If, however, the enquirer is totally insincere, then remain silent as Jesus did and commit your case to the righteous judge.

29

THE CRUCIFIXION

Countless volumes have been written on the death of Christ, and Paul comments that it will take all eternity for us to learn the riches of the grace of God towards us in Christ Jesus. A short study can never do justice to the central event of all time.

The Lord suffered most cruelly. He endured six examinations, none of which was fair and in none of which was He shown any courtesy or kindness. He was mocked and struck repeatedly. He was flogged—a punishment that many did not survive. He probably got no sleep, and He had no food or drink over quite a prolonged period. Thirst can be an agonising symptom; and hence, His cry on the cross and His extreme dehydration may explain why His death was so rapid.

Contemporary writings by Roman and Greek writers describe crucifixions in detail, dwelling on the extreme tortures, the incredible sufferings of the victims, and the humiliation of exposure to public ridicule and mockery. Scripture, however, is almost silent on all such details. The overall impression from the records is of the dignity of Jesus and His concern for those around Him: the women of Jerusalem (Luke 23: 27–31, NIV); Simon the Cyrenian, who probably became a Christian (see Mark 15: 21, NIV; Rom. 16: 13, NIV); Pilate; Mary, His mother, and John (John 19: 25–27, NIV); and the repentant thief (Luke 23: 39–43, NIV). His prayer for forgiveness for His tormentors also shows His concern for others and not Himself (Luke 23: 34, NIV). The aim of the gospel writers is to stimulate our worship and not our pity, our wonder at divine love and not human suffering. As the writer to the Hebrews puts it (12: 2, NIV), Jesus Himself ignored the shame of the cross and focused on the joy that would follow His sufferings and death.

It has been pointed out that the largest number of apparent differences among the four gospels occur in the accounts of the crucifixion. This, however, is fully consistent with their truthfulness. John was the only gospel writer who actually witnessed the crucifixion, and he did not even watch it to the end. So how do we have any of the details given in the four gospels? Clearly, these must have come from eyewitness and hence the suggestion that some, perhaps a number of those who had been involved in the event, later became Christians.

It has been suggested that the account in Matthew may be based on evidence given by a Jewish priest who had become a Christian. Mark and Luke too must have got their material from onlookers who later became followers. Edersheim (*The Life and Times of Jesus the Messiah*—a pure gold commentary!) even suggests that the centurion who had been in charge of the crucifixion may have been Luke's informant. Undoubtedly the differences among the accounts—none of which is of any theological importance—could easily be resolved had we more detailed information.

Yet again we note that the aim of the writers is not to focus on the human elements in the events but on the love of Christ for fallen man and the redemption He was procuring for us.

One remarkable item in these events is the fulfilment of a number of prophecies, which had been written hundreds of years earlier. Some of these are utterly remarkable. John records the ghastly fact that the soldiers broke the legs of the two thieves in order to hasten their death, but they did not do this to Jesus. The witness who told John about this related it with surprise, and he then went on to record with amazement that a soldier had pierced the Lord's side. What a despicable and senseless thing to do to a body that was already dead.

But as John recorded this, he remembered that all this had been predicted (John 19: 36, 37, NIV), one part 2,000 years before and the other 600 years previously. In Exodus 12: 46 it is stated that no bone of the Passover sacrifice was to be broken, and Christ is our Passover (1 Cor. 5: 7, NIV).

Zechariah 12: 10 (NIV) and 13: 7 refer to the Messiah being pierced. Psalm 22: 16 (NIV) also foretold the piercing of His hands and feet. Another prophecy in Psalm 22: 18 (NIV) refers to how the soldiers would divide the garments of Jesus.

At the end of his book, John states his reason for recording all this: the fulfilment of these prophecies is very powerful evidence of the dependability of scripture as the word of God and powerful evidence of the deity of Jesus. As John says, 'I have written these things so that you will believe that Jesus is the Christ, the Son of God, and that believing you might have life in Him' (John 20: 30, 31, NIV).

Perhaps, however, the most remarkable thing of all is how the Lord's concern seems to have been focused on others. He looked lightly on his suffering and his humiliation—for the joy that was set before him. That joy was ultimately the relationships with himself into which men and women would be brought on the basis of his sufferings and death. But even in his dying, he seems to have been concerned to initiate relationships with those around him.

There was Simon from Cyprus. He had had to help carry the cross, a terrible indignity, for a visitor to the city. But why does Mark add that Simon is the father of Rufus and Alexander? Of what possible interest is this unless, of course, the two sons were known to the infant church. It takes little imagination to wonder if Simon became a Christian on the basis of his brief contact with Jesus.

Then there was the centurion. Tradition says his name was Longisimus. Was it he, or was it one of the soldiers who gave John the details about their gambling? And what about the details of the request to Pilate and the horrific events that followed (John 19: 31–34, NIV)?

These details sound like the witness of the centurion. Surely he became a Christian.

Then there was the dying thief who had perhaps known something of Jesus ('This man has done nothing amiss') but who was so moved by what he saw of the Lord's attitude towards his tormentors that he became a believer.

Later, Jesus told Peter how he would die, and John added that Jesus told him this 'signifying by what death he [Peter] would glorify God' (John 21: 19, NIV). Here, in the Lord's concern for others around him at the crucifixion, we see how the Lord himself showed the glory of God in his dying.

But the deepest concern of the Lord was for his mother (John 19: 26, 27, NIV). Jesus knew the agonies a mother would suffer on losing a son. And so he made loving provision for her.

> *This was preached in Temple on 18 February 1998, a few days after a visiting pastor and his wife who were working with the church had lost their premature son. Also in the congregation was another mother who had lost her infant daughter a few weeks previously. The last point above seems to have been of God-given applicability. The talk at the funeral of one of the infants had focused on the statement of David about the infant son he had lost: 'He will not return to me but I will go to him.'*

> *The sermon on the crucifixion ended with what might be called the mirror image of this statement by David: 'I will see you again, your heart will rejoice and no man will take away your joy' (John 16: 22, NIV). He is with us in sorrows and in bereavement. He is with you, and no man will take away that joy.*

John also mentions blood and water flowing from the spear wound. There have been several explanations of this; but the most reasonable would seem to be that death had occurred, the circulation had stopped, and the red cells and serum had separated. The spear then probably pierced the heart. This is important because some have tried to argue that Jesus never died. In fact, in addition to this evidence, there is the testimony of the Roman centurion (Mark 15: 44, 45, NIV). Palestine was a tough assignment for the occupying force, and the Romans sent hardened, experienced men. The centurion will have known his job, and he would have forfeited his own life had he not completed the task given to him.

Matthew and Mark both record that the veil of the Temple was mysteriously torn when the Saviour died. This is highly significant for a number of reasons. First, it was ripped from the top, consistent with a work of God. Second, that veil had prevented men coming into the presence of the glory of God in the holiest place within the Temple. Now, one in whom dwelt the fullness of the godhead bodily (Col. 2: 9, NIV) opened up a new and living way to God 'through the veil, that is to say, His flesh (Heb. 10: 20, NIV).

30

THE DEATH OF CHRIST

At Athens Paul spoke to the Greeks about their philosophy and attempted to argue Christianity from their writers. He had little success. He travelled on to Corinth and arrived there in deep depression, saddened perhaps by his failure at Athens. He wrote later about this and said, 'I determined to know nothing among you, but Christ crucified' (1 Cor. 2: 2, NIV). The simple message of the gospel was enough.

And yet the gospel is no simple matter. Scripture uses many human concepts in attempts to explain something of the profound mystery of the death of the Son of God and its effects on us. Scripture also uses pictures in attempting to convey aspects of the death of Jesus: Passover, the sin and the trespass offerings, the offering of the red heifer, the atonement offering, etc. These sacrifices should be studied as should the ceremony of atonement (Lev. 16) as they will enrich our understanding of the death of Christ. The bottom line, however, is as Paul wrote: 'It will take all eternity for God to show us the riches of His grace towards us in Christ Jesus' (Eph. 2: 7, NIV).

REDEMPTION: Ancient customs provided for the deliverance of slaves by the payment of a ransom and for the buying back of an inheritance that had been lost. These are both known as redemption. They go beyond deliverance in that, first, there was always a cost and, second, only a blood relative, and not anyone, could redeem a person who had lost his freedom or an inheritance that had been lost. Indeed, the Hebrew word for a relative or kinsman, is 'one who can redeem'.

By human birth, Jesus Christ became a kinsman of ours, related to us so that He could pay the price of our redemption.

COVENANT: In all human societies, there has been provision for a formal agreement or covenant between two or more parties. In grace, God has made covenants with men. For example, He agreed not to send another flood and He gave a sign of this covenant: the rainbow (see Gen. 9: 8–17, NIV). He made a covenant with Abraham with circumcision as the sign (Gen. 15: 6–21, 17: 9–10, NIV). In His death, Jesus established 'a new covenant' in His own blood; and the cup taken at communion is the sign.

Notice, however, that although in most covenants men enter into an agreement as equals, God takes the initiative and every covenant of His is 'by grace'. There are, however, obligations and responsibilities with every covenant; and so we are urged to 'examine ourselves' as to our Christian walk whenever we take the cup in communion (1 Cor. 11: 28, NIV).

PROPITIATION: This is a difficult concept. The word means to appease and has been used to describe the pathetic sacrifices, which some offer in attempting to placate their gods. God is infinitely holy, and the Bible warns that nothing that man can do can appease the anger and the judgement of God against sin. Jesus Christ, however, is the propitiation for us (Rom. 3: 25, NIV) in that His sacrifice appeases the anger of God against sin. By His death, the holiness and the righteousness of God are preserved.

The concept of propitiation is closely connected with the idea of 'covering', and the word is used for the mercy seat within the tabernacle and temple. Exodus 25: 17–20 (NIV) explains how a 'mercy seat' of pure gold was to be made to cover the ark, within which the tables of stone, the law, was to be kept. Over the ark, there were to be two angels or cherubim, and their faces were to look towards the mercy seat, under which the law was kept.

On each Day of Atonement, the blood of a sacrifice was to be sprinkled on the mercy seat (Lev. 16: 14, NIV); and this meant that the cherubim, the executors of God's justice, instead of seeing the law, the basis of God's judgement, they saw the blood of a sacrifice and the judgement of God based on the law was held back.

> Come, Thou Fount Of Every Blessing, Tune My Heart
> To Sing Thy Grace; He, To Save My Soul From Danger,
> Interposed His Precious Blood.

RECONCILIATION: The words used for this are those for exchanging money i.e. changing one currency into another. Men are to exchange anger for mercy, and they are to be reconciled to one another by 'meeting in the middle' (Matt. 5: 23–26, NIV). A different wording, however, is used with reference to God. Man is commanded to be reconciled to God. All the change is to be on man's part. God is changeless and cannot compromise in order to meet man in the middle! The earliest use of this concept with reference to man and God is by Job: 'O that there were one between us, who could lay a hand upon us both and bring us together (Job 9: 32–35, NIV).

JUSTIFICATION: This is a legal term. When a court declares a man justified, from then on, he is to be considered never to have committed the offence with which he had been charged. His record is clean. From Abraham onwards, justification is the legal declaration in scripture of those who express faith in Jesus Christ. Notice that some terms for salvation can be expressed as a process. For example, we have been saved from the guilt of sin, we are being saved from the power of sin, and we will be saved from the presence of sin. 'Christ delivered us, and doth deliver us, and we trust will yet deliver us' (2 Cor. 1: 10, NIV). On the other hand, justification, being a declaration about the forgiveness of the Christian, is always stated in the past tense. We have been justified.

All these concepts are freely used throughout the New Testament, usually singly, but occasionally several are used together. For example, in Romans 3 Paul speaks of the universal need of man (23) and the complete provision by God (24 and 25). He refers to this last as man '*justified* by His grace, through *redemption* in Christ, who is the *propitiation* for our sins'. Paul then adds a most significant comment: in this way, God justifies the sinner and at the same time remains just Himself. Anything less would either leave sinners unforgiven or would compromise God's own holiness.

31

THE DEATH OF CHRIST:
THE JEWISH SACRIFICES

Crucifixion was designed by the Phoenicians and developed by the Romans so as to inflict the greatest possible sufferings on a man.

The basic situation is clear: a holy and pure God, on the one hand, and sinful man on the other. How can the two be brought together? Not by God compromising—He would be no longer God—but by man being cleansed and made fit for a relationship with God. This is not simple. A solution has to be provided by God and appropriated by man. The animal sacrifices in the Old Testament help us in understanding the various aspects of the work of Jesus. Study of the sacrifices will enrich our understanding, deepen our worship, and enrich our relationship with Christ.

PASSOVER (Exod. 12. NIV): To the Jews, Passover speaks of deliverance. They had been slaves in Egypt. God said He would deliver them, He would make them a nation of great consequence, He would work out His purposes through them, and He would bring them into an inheritance. Central to Passover was the slaying of a lamb. They were to fully identify with that lamb; and so the lamb was, as it were, to become part of them. Hence, they had to eat the lamb. Its blood, however, was to be sprinkled; and when the angel of death, sent by

113

God, saw the blood, he would pass over. Jesus is our Passover (2 Cor. 5: 21, NIV). He fulfilled this sacrifice in its minutest detail.

THE SIN AND THE TRESPASS OFFERINGS (Lev. 4, NIV): An Israelite who had sinned could maintain His communion with God only if he confessed his sin and it was covered, and he had been ceremonially cleansed. The man would take an animal, confess his sin over its head, and they slay it. God had said, 'The soul that sins must die.' The death of the animal counted for his own. Jesus fulfilled this sacrifice, dying in our place.

THE DAY OF ATONEMENT (Lev. 16, NIV): On one day each year, Israel was to make 'atonement' (literally, a covering) for their sins. This was to be preceded by the people examining themselves and confessing their sin. On the special day, the high priest would offer a sin offering for himself to fit himself to mediate between God and the people. (Note: Hebrews 9: 12 [NIV] points out that Christ did not do this as He was sinless.) The priest then confessed the sins of the people over the head of one of the two animals and slew it. Taking some of the blood, he entered the most holy place in the Temple and sprinkled it on the mercy seat over the Ark of the Covenant. The second animal was to be a 'scapegoat'. The sins of the people were to be confessed over it; and it was to be driven away into the wilderness, carrying the sins of the people as it were, never to be seen again (Lev. 16: 10, NIV). This is all rich in symbolism—all fulfilled in Christ (see Heb. 9, NIV).

THE RED HEIFER (Num. 19, NIV): This is the most unusual of all the sacrifices, yet it speaks dramatically of certain aspects of Christ's death in a way that no other sacrifice does. A spotless heifer in its prime was to be burnt. The ashes were to be stored and used later in cleansing defilement. This speaks of the ongoing value of the death of Jesus. If I sin, He does not have to die again. There is 'stored up' merit in His death. If the ashes of a heifer sprinkling the unclean sanctifieth to the purifying of the flesh, how much more shall the bleed of Christ purge your conscience from dead works to service the living God (Heb. 9: 13, NIV)?

There were two groups of sacrifices. Those to do with sin were burnt wholly to ashes. The word used implies a fierce fire, symbolic of the wrath of God towards sin. The other group of sacrifices were associated with a love of God and worship. The words used for them include 'a sweet savour offering', and they are said to 'ascend to God'. Understanding of these should enhance our worship of God.

THE BURNT OFFERING (Lev. 1, NIV): A man could bring an animal and offer it to God out of love and gratitude. Special mention is made of the head, the legs, and the innards of the animal; and this suggests that the worshipper was to examine his own thoughts (head), his walk (the legs), his attitude, and his emotions (the innards). The death of Christ is spoken of as 'a burnt offering, well pleasing to God' (Eph. 5: 2, NIV). No surprise! But what is surprising, and thrilling, is that the service we do to others in the name of Christ is spoken of as a 'a fragrant offering, an acceptable sacrifice, well pleasing to God' (Phil 4:18 NIV).

THE PEACE OFFERING (Lev. 7: 11, NIV): This is a most interesting sacrifice. If a man wanted to make up a quarrel and really put it behind him, he could offer a peace offering. Part of the animal was sacrificed on the altar to God, and part was given to be eaten by the priests. The rest of the animal had to be consumed that same day. This meant that the man had to call his friends together (hopefully including the one with whom he had quarrelled), and they had a feast. If relationships are to be good and healthy, God must be central. We must share with friends and fellow Christians; and if there has been a quarrel, it is best healed and relationships restored over a meal!

THE RESURRECTION: - (I) THE STORY

It was early morning, and a small group of women walked quickly and quietly through the dark streets. Several of them were carrying heavy loads of ointment. They were tired. They had been up most of the night, grinding and mixing the spices and making them into a paste. Once the Sabbath sun had set, they had started and had worked most of the night. They hurried to one of the eastern gates, knowing it would be open. They had timed their journey so that they would not have to wait. They passed through quickly and hurried along the road outside. They turned in off the road and through a little gate into a garden. They proceeded nervously, much slower now. Rumour had it that there had been soldiers around, but they saw nobody as they advanced cautiously.

And then they stopped, quite taken aback. They had come to a rock face where the tomb was, and they saw that the stone had been moved away from the entrance. The thought of that huge stone had worried them. They had watched late one evening a few days before, and they had seen the body hastily wrapped for burial. They had cringed as they had watched the men handle the body. That was woman's work. The men had been so clumsy and insensitive, yet the women had been afraid to interfere. One didn't speak to a member of the Sanhedrin—certainly not a woman! Now they had come to make good the omissions of the men and hence all the ointment they had prepared during the night and had brought with them now.

And here they were. The tomb open and no guard. What a relief. So they went forward confidently and bent low as they entered the tomb. Once inside, they groped round in the dark. It was impossible to see, and they had no idea of the size of the tomb or its shape or anything. Their pulses rose, their breathing became short, they gasped—the tomb was empty. The grave clothes were still there but no body. One of them continued to grope around. Was there a hidden chamber, a shelf perhaps? The others went outside. They talked excitedly, distraught at the missing body.

And then suddenly, from nowhere, two men appeared. They were startled, thinking them to be the guards; but despite the darkness, they could see these men quite clearly. They seemed to be quite bright, shining even. The women were terrified, and some of them fell about. If they weren't guards, who were they? They hardly listened as the men spoke to them. They were so frightened, though one or two of the women did question them. They went on about things Jesus had said while he had been alive, but they were so frightened. They practically fled the garden after that; and they started to run back, calling to one another that they would tell the men. They would know what to do. And so they set off for Mark's home, knowing some of the men would be there.

But then Mary remembered the ointment. The others were all for leaving it, but Mary couldn't forget all the work that had gone into preparing it, and so she insisted that she would go back. None of the others would go; but she said she would wait until those men—whoever they were—had gone, and then she would hide the ointment in the bushes.

Meanwhile, back in Jerusalem, the guards were arguing with the centurion. He was absolutely furious. The men had deserted their post—unthinkable for a Roman soldier. But the men they sent to this dreadful posting in Jerusalem were the dregs of the army. What could you expect? Certainly not loyalty!

And yet the centurion himself was uneasy. The whole business had been odd from the start. Crucifixion was always a nasty job, but it had to be done. He had seen many, and he had always got on with it and got it over as quickly as possible. But that man had been different. His attitude—the way He hadn't responded to all the jeers and the mocking, the way he had spoken to one of the other poor wretches.

Yet rules were rules, and these deserters were for the chop—all of them. And, well, they deserved it! But to whom should he report them? They were Roman soldiers, but they had been under Jewish orders when they had been on duty at that tomb. He hastily scribbled a note and called a messenger to take it to the Jewish authorities.

The women had become quite angry with the men. They were in Mark's house, and all Peter kept saying was 'Shush, you'll wake the others.' Peter said they were all hysterical, or they had gone to the wrong tomb; but in the end, he had called John, and he had agreed to go and check, provided John came with him.

So the two men set out along the same road the women had taken, out through the eastern gate, and into the garden. By then, John was running; and not to lose sight of him, Peter lumbered along behind. Mary heard them coming; and thinking that they were the guards returning, she hid down low behind the bushes where she had been hiding the ointment. The men ran up to the tomb, barely noticing that the stone had been moved aside. John stooped down and looked in, keeping to one side not to block the early morning light. No doubt about it. The grave clothes were there, but they were lying flat; and clearly, there was no body. Then Peter, the big clumsy fellow, ran up; and his momentum carried him right into the tomb. Not very bright either. He lifted up the grave clothes as if there could have been a body underneath! And he even looked into the complicated windings, stiff with ointment, that had been around the head of the body. The clumsy oaf—no respect for the dead!

And then it hit John! All those grave clothes. They had been wrapped up until Peter had disturbed them. Still wound up. Not cut or torn in pieces. Wrapped tightly together and lying apart from the other clothes.

They walked away in silence, each deep in thought: Peter wondering about the body, John puzzling about the grave clothes and trying to make sense of some of the things Jesus had said to them before it had all happened.

Meantime, back in the corridors of power, a few of the Jewish leaders were talking intently with the centurion. They were pleading with him to bring the guards out of the cells and let them talk to them. Reluctantly, the centurion agreed; and slipping the 100 denaria note under his robes, he went down to the cells to release the men.

The centurion was astounded to see the friendly way the Jewish leaders greeting the soldiers—slimy and fawning he would have called it! And then they went on to ask the deserters if they had not seen some of the followers of the man come and take his body away. No, of course not, they protested. They were not afraid of any man, let alone any of you, Jews! A few more 100 denaria notes seemed to change hands, and the guards agreed that they had probably fallen asleep while the disciples had taken the body.

Well, that was too much for the centurion. He intervened and angrily pointed out that the guards were Romans, and no Roman ever slept on duty. That was going too far! But those Jews—they had thought of everything; and as the centurion was tucking a few more denaria notes under his robes, the Jews explained to him that there were lots more where those had come from and they would settle Pilate if ever he heard about the matter.

Mary had been terrified when she had heard the guards, as she had thought the men to be, running though the garden. But they hadn't seen her or the ointment. So as soon as they had gone, Mary completed her work and started to leave the garden to return home.

But just one last look, she thought, just in case they had been mistaken. And so she returned to the tomb; and stooping down, she looked in. Poor Mary! She nearly jumped out of her skin when a shadow of a man fell across the entrance. She turned and recovered somewhat when she saw that the man was clearly no soldier. Possible a gardener, she thought, and so she started to ask him about the body. She was so tearful and distraught that she rambled on about carrying the body away herself.

The man just said one word: 'Mary'. It was He! No one else had ever said her name like that! Others had said her name coldly, and some with a sneer, knowing her past. But He had always said it with such love and warmth. It was Him all right! She flung herself at Him and grasped His feet.

Well, the rest of that morning was sheer chaos! Word spread quickly, but it wasn't a clear message that got round. Many heard about the tomb being empty; and they went—some alone, some in pairs, some again and again—checking repeatedly. Then there was Peter, who wanted to organise a search party for body, but no one would listen to him. And no one could get a sensible word out of John. He was in one of his trances, and he kept muttering about the grave clothes and repeating over and over some of the things Jesus had said over supper before it had all happened. And Mary—she was like one who had seen a vision, except it had been no vision. She was so clear and definite about every detail.

And it was all resolved that same evening:

> *The same day, at evening, when the doors were shut where the disciples were assembled for fear of the Jews, came Jesus and*

stood in the midst of them and said: 'Peace be unto you.' And when he had so said, he showed them His hands and His side. Then were the disciples glad when they saw their Lord. Then Jesus said to them again: 'Peace be unto you. As the Father sent me, even so send I you.' (John 20: 19–21, NIV)

33

THE RESURRECTION - (II) THE EVIDENCE

In his first letter to the Christians at Corinth, written very soon after Jesus had died, Paul makes the claim that Jesus had risen; and then he says, 'Over 500 people who met Jesus after he had risen from the dead are still alive.' It is as if he is saying, 'Go and talk to them if you have any doubts!' Of course, all those witnesses are dead and cannot now be cross-examined. But that is to miss the point. The value of the statement Paul made is that what he wrote about the resurrection could have been—and would have been—thoroughly checked. It is therefore reasonable to presume that if the facts he gives had been incorrect in any detail, the letter would have been rubbished and would not have survived. The same is, of course, true for all the gospel records.

THE SOLDIERS' STORY: The first to acknowledge that something had happened to the body of Jesus were the enemies of Jesus. Matthew records that the guards at the tomb reported that there had been an earthquake, the tomb had opened, and the body of Jesus had disappeared! The authorities were alarmed, so they bribed the soldiers to say that they had all fallen asleep and the disciples had stolen the body. What nonsense! A Roman soldier who slept on duty could be put to death. Perhaps that is why Matthew adds the little detail that they had to be heavily bribed. The Jewish authorities must have been desperate if they were willing to pay money liberally!

DID JESUS REALLY DIE? Some have argued that Jesus only fainted on the cross and that in the cool of the tomb he revived, got out, and met again with his followers. The suggestion has no conviction. The soldiers who had conducted the crucifixion had been convinced of His death and had not broken His legs as they had done with the two thieves. One of them had pierced the Saviour's side, and blood and water (presumably serum and red cells) had flowed. The Roman governor had sent for the centurion who had been in charge of the crucifixion to obtain an assurance that Jesus was dead. Then if Jesus had come to within the tomb, He would have had to free Himself from the many metres of grave clothes that would have been wrapped tightly around His body, smeared with many kilos of ointment. The heavy stone over the entrance and the soldiers watching outside would have had to have been overcome. And after all this, how could a faint nine-tenths dead spectre convince his followers and lead them to face the authorities and start to turn the world upside down as it was later claimed they were doing?

THE WOMEN'S STORY: Luke tells how some women were the first to find the tomb empty. They were distraught, and they ran to find some of the men. The men reacted as men should! They dismissed the women's story as idle tales! But the men were no fools. They checked, and they found things exactly as the women had said. Now that is all important. One or two people might have had a hallucination, especially in a garden in the half light of the early morning. But would hard men be fooled when the sun was up? And what about the 500 witnesses, all of whom had met Jesus and were available later for cross-examination?

THE EVIDENCE IN THE TOMB: In chapter 20, John tells how he had gone to the garden with Peter. He had actually gone into the tomb and had inspected it! He first noticed that there was something strange about the grave clothes—so strange that he examined them closely. His description implies they were all still wrapped up; and the napkin that had been around the head of Jesus was lying, collapsed, just as it would have been had the body been inside. Had Jesus revived, the burial cloths would have been strewn around; or had grave robbers visited the tomb, the cloths would have gone. In fact, this evidence of something unusual about the cloths was so powerful that John adds in his account that it led him to believe in Jesus!

The most powerful evidence from the tomb is that it was empty. It is utterly remarkable that after that first morning, during which the followers of Jesus seemed to have dashed backwards and forwards to the garden, the tomb was never mentioned again. Not for six centuries is there another reference to the grave of Jesus. Strange, when the tomb of almost every other world leader and every other person of note has become a place of pilgrimage. The tomb of Stalin, Mohamed, and Buddha can all be visited. But the tomb of Jesus was of no interest to his followers; and it wasn't until Catherine, 600 years later, sent an expedition to Jerusalem that any interest was shown in the site or, rather, the possible site because to this day it is not known for certain where the tomb was.

WHAT ABOUT THE BODY? In any murder trial, a crucial matter is evidence about the body: Where is the body. What does it show? More so in this situation than in any murder trial! Had the Jewish authorities produced the body of Jesus, all the claims about his resurrection would have been stopped—finally and permanently!

THE FOLLOWERS OF JESUS: Jesus had been a remarkable leader, but he had chosen a strange group of successors. He had toured Israel with a little group of uneducated men with little gift between them: a few fishermen, a tax inspector, and a few others with nothing exceptional about them. Yet a short time later, the civil authorities complained that the followers of Jesus were turning the world upside down! Two points emerge. First, what changed those men? Something unusual, even stupendous, must have happened to them. But second, all those who taught and who wrote about the Christian message urged honesty and integrity—even if it meant death. And most of them did die for what they taught. Could they have faced death for a lie? And even more unlikely, could they have urged their followers and the readers of their writings to die for a lie or for something that was only wishful thinking? No way! Men just are not like that!

34

THE RISEN LORD AND HIS FOLLOWERS

John 21 is a remarkable chapter. Whereas both John 20 and all the other gospel records focus on the pieces of evidence for the resurrection and the various appearances of the risen Lord, John 21 (NIV) is very different. It appears to indicate how the Lord, now that He is risen, will operate with his followers. He is about to leave the disciples, but first He demonstrates how He will continue to love and care for them after He has physically departed from them.

The risen Lord watches over those who follow Him (4): During the three years, Jesus had been with the disciples. He had led then and provided for them; and as far as we know, he had never left them. Now He is about to leave them; and as far as the material world goes, his departure will be permanent. At the tomb, He had told Mary, 'Don't touch me' (literally, 'Don't cling to me'), implying that the relationship he would now have with her, and with all his followers, would not be in the physical realm but would be in the heart and mind. For this same reason, he had spoken in the upper room of his 'indwelling' those who loved him.

And so the Lord gave a demonstration of this kind of relationship operating at a distance. He had told the women to give the disciples instructions to go to Galilee before him. Galilee was a very large province with a huge lake. How would he meet up with them there? Yet one morning, there he was, watching them from the shore of the lake (4). And thus, he demonstrated how, although he would soon be absent from them physically, he would know exactly where they were and what they were doing. So after he would leave them physically, he would continue to watch over them. So it is for us!

The risen Lord guides those who follow Him (6): Some have been critical of the disciples for the way that as soon as they got back to Galilee they went back to fishing. Surely, they had been called by Christ and had left their trades. Should they not have waited for him? But is such a view reasonable? There was no rebuke from Jesus. And elsewhere, the Bible commends work and condemns those who can but do not work.

More than that, the Lord guided the disciples in their fishing. He directed them from a distance; and in following their Lord's directions, the disciples had unusual success (6). So it is for us!

The risen Lord provides for those who follow Him (9): Verse 9 reads strangely. The fishermen return to land, dragging their huge catch; and they find that Jesus already has fish cooking for them! Where did he get them? Ultimately, of course, he is the provider. He knows our every need, and everything we have comes from him.

The risen Lord values what His followers do under His guidance (10): The Lord of creation stands at a fire he has lit, cooking the fish he has provided. In grace, however, he tells the disciples to bring some of the fish they have caught. Why? Could he not supply enough? Of course, he could! But in grace he valued what the disciples had done, and in grace he used some of their catch. So it is with us. The Lord of the universe could achieve his purposes, but in grace he delegates to us and involves us, and he values whatever we do for him.

The risen Lord forgives and restores those who fall (15–17, NIV): Peter had failed the Lord badly, and his denials had been silenced by the crowing of a cock. Luke tells us that following this, the Lord had looked at Peter. Luke doesn't say what was in that look, but we can imagine the love and understanding Jesus conveyed to Peter. We then read that after his resurrection, Jesus appeared to Peter alone. No doubt there was confession and forgiveness at that meeting. But that had all been private, between Jesus and Peter alone. Now Jesus makes his forgiveness clear to all the disciples. And more than that, Jesus restores their relationship openly; and in front of the others, he delegates to Peter a special task.

So it is for us! When we fail him, there is forgiveness. The relationship can be restored. But more than this, our failures and the experience of his forgiveness and restoration can fit us to be a help and encouragement to others.

The risen Lord knows our end and will be with us through the valley of death (18–22, NIV): Jesus, knowing all things, was frank with Peter; and he gently described the suffering and violent death Peter would have to face. But John added a remarkable phrase to the Lord's description of Peter's death, saying that in the way he would face death and would die, Peter would 'glorify God'. A remarkable phrase. Death is distressing; and yet, a follower of Jesus can 'glorify' the one who has promised to be with us through (and not just into) the valley of the shadow of death in the way he meets death and handles the pain, the suffering, and the distress of separation.

> *Perhaps one of the most thrilling aspect of this last point is the confidence Peter showed at the end of his life. He knew that he was to die a horrible death, and tradition has it that he was crucified upside down. Yet Peter wrote about his end calmly, referring to how he would shortly 'put off the tent of this body' and would have 'an abundant entrance' (or 'a rich welcome') into the eternal kingdom of our Lord and Saviour.*
> (2 Pet. 1: 11–14, NIV)

35

THE RESURRECTED LORD

Not just the body of Jesus rose at the resurrection,
all His promises and all His claims rose with Him.

Archbishop Ramsay wrote the above. That is, had Jesus died and stayed dead, no one would probably have heard of Him now, and certainly no one would be too bothered about Him. He and all His teachings would be totally forgotten. But He is not forgotten! No one in the history of man has had such a profound and lasting effect upon society and not just in the so-called Western world. His followers are growing rapidly throughout the world. No general, no politician, no scientist has had an effect upon society that can remotely compare with that of Jesus Christ.

The resurrection means that the claims Jesus made—indeed, everything He said and did—must be taken very seriously. He made claims to deity, to absolute knowledge, to infinite power. He claimed that He will judge every man and that the attitude of men to Him will determine their destiny after death. These are all either the claims of a madman or a hoaxer—or they are true! These are the only alternatives. Yet nothing about Him remotely suggests that either He was a rogue or a fool.

Of course, most of the claims Jesus made cannot be tested. What He said about His origin cannot be tested. In the nature of things, we cannot have evidence about the things he said about the future. There can therefore be no certainty about what Jesus said about judgement and heaven and hell. At least, there can be no certainty until we are there, and it is too late!

It is here that the statement that 'not just the body of Jesus rose' is so helpful. Any fool can make claims that cannot be tested; but if someone claims that they will rise from the dead, then just wait and see! Time will reveal pretty clearly and decisively whether or not he is a fool or a rogue!

It is a fact that the only thing in life of which we can have absolute certainty is that one day each of us will die. Strange therefore that most of us don't bother to think much about death. It is all so morbid that we keep putting it out of our mind! But if someone claims to have returned from the dead and to be able to tell us all about death and about what follows, then surely it is the strangest thing of all if folk don't want to listen. If you are not sure where you are going, ask a man who does!

Before He died and rose, Jesus talked a lot to his followers about heaven and hell. He said that he could give eternal life to those who ask Him to be their Saviour, those who ask Him to forgive their sins, to cleanse them, and to come into their heart and life as Saviour and Lord. He promised that all who come to Him in this way would be His and that one day He would take all of them to be with Him forever.

But Jesus also warned that any man who rejects Him and the truth he taught will have to stand before Him as judge one day and answer for his response to his offer of salvation. Perhaps the most awful thing that Jesus will say on that day will be 'You made your choice when you were alive. You decided you didn't want Me. I now give you your choice for all eternity. Depart from Me!'

On the other hand, those who ask the Lord Jesus for forgiveness and ask Him to be their Saviour and their Lord will be saved and will be taken by Him to be with Him for all eternity, and that is just as dependable as the fact that Jesus rose from the dead on that first Easter morning!

The death of Jesus opened a new way to God.
Hebrews 10: 20 refers to this as 'a living way' because He lives!
Peter 1: 3 states that those who take that way
have 'a living hope' because He lives!

CODICIL

THE ASCENSION
(ACTS 1: 1-11, NIV)

Someone has said that 'Christians live between the times of his comings'. Jesus came to earth in the incarnation. He returned to heaven, but he promised that he would come back, and he added, 'Blessed is that servant whom his master finds waiting, watching and working for him' (Matt. 24: 46, NIV).

The account in Acts has, of course, its difficulties. It is said that when Jesus left this earth, he went up into the sky and was obscured by a cloud (Acts 1: 9, NIV). Strange, when we all know that heaven isn't up there. On the other hand, there had to be a very definite close to the earthly phase of the life of Jesus. The disciples had been totally dependent upon Jesus; and during four years, he had been everything to them. Furthermore, following the resurrection, he had appeared suddenly on a number of occasions. Now they would have to stand on their own feet. That phase of their relationship had to be brought to a very clear and obvious end; and so Jesus made use of their concept of heaven as 'up there', and he ascended and disappeared into a cloud.

Following his ascension, the disciples were told to stay in Jerusalem (Acts 1: 4, NIV). Why? They had all failed in Jerusalem. They had fled on the arrest of Jesus, and even the news of his resurrection had caused them to behave as confused and frightened men. It would have been easy for them to have gone away and make a new start elsewhere.

131

But Jesus wanted them to face their failure—and to do more than face things! He wanted them to turn the tide and reverse the hostility and opposition that had led to his death. And so the first successes of his followers were to be there, among the people and the religious leaders who had hounded Jesus to his death (Acts 2: 41, 6: 7, NIV).

Furthermore, perhaps the greatest single event of failure had been in Jerusalem. Peter had denied knowledge of Jesus in the house of the high priest. That had to be reversed. And so Peter was given a second chance; and within a short time, he courageously witnessed to his knowledge of Jesus before the Sanhedrin (Acts 4: 13, NIV).

We too can run away from failures; or we can face them, sort out the damage, and learn from them.

There is, of course, a basic reason for his departure from earth. Jesus had said that he had to go so that the Holy Spirit could come. The Spirit of God is described as *holy*; and if he is to 'indwell' the followers of Jesus, then a means of cleansing from sin had first to be made available. So the death of Jesus was a necessary preliminary to the coming of the Holy Spirit and his indwelling in this new way.

The disciples were also told that 'this same Jesus will come back in the same way as he has ascended' (Acts 1: 11, NIV). Is this to be taken literally? Is Jesus going to appear physically one day in the sky?

While there are a number of views on details of the return of Christ at the end of the age, there can be no doubt that he will come back and will execute justice and judgement and set up his everlasting kingdom. Jesus took his physical body, risen and glorified by resurrection, into heaven; and so presumably 'this same Jesus' will return in that same body. Therefore, 'every eye will see him', 'his feet will stand on the Mount of Olives', and some will have to look at 'him whom they pierced' (Zech. 12: 10, 14: 4, NIV).

But the mystery of all this is even deeper! Scripture seems to indicate that the followers of Jesus will have bodies like his (2 Cor. 5: 1–10 [NIV], 1 John 3: 2 [NIV]); and it will be in these that they will serve and worship him in 'the new heaven and earth, wherein dwelleth righteousness' (2 Pet. 3: 13, NIV).

Over the years, there have been arguments and divisions over details of the return of Christ. While scripture implies that we should read the scriptures that refer to this, we should not be too concerned over details. Jesus himself gave us the basic principle for the interpretation of prophecy: 'I tell you now, so that when it comes to pass you will know that I AM' (John 13: 19, NIV). When the events of the end begin to unfold, there will be no argument!

For the Christians, the bottom line of all this is that there is a man in the glory! Jesus is in heaven, interceding for those who are his, sustaining their faith, and preparing a place for them. At death, he will be there and will give them 'a rich welcome' into his everlasting kingdom (2 Pet. 1: 11, NIV). At the end of the age, he will return to earth with them and will achieve the purposes for which he had originally created the earth and the universe, the fulfilment of which has been delayed by sin and rebellion. Then, in grace, he will involve those who have trusted in him as Saviour and Lord in working out his great and eternal purposes.

Scripture clearly implies that how we live for him now and how we use our abilities and our opportunities for him will determine the part each of us will play in the working out of his great and eternal purposes (2 Cor. 5: 10, NIV).

> *Each one should be careful how he builds. For no one can lay any foundation other than the one already laid, which is Jesus Christ. If any man builds on this foundation using gold, silver, costly stones, wood, hay or straw, his work will be shown for what it is, because the day will bring it to light. It will be revealed with fire, and the fire will test the quality of each man's work. If what he has built survives, he will receive his reward. If it is burned up, he will suffer loss; he himself will be saved, but only as one escaping through the flames.* (1 Cor. 3: 11–15, NIV).

> *'If a man would live well, let him fetch his last day to him and make it always his company keeper'* (The Interpreter, *Pilgrim's Progress*)